on track ...

Aimee Mann

every album, every song

Jez Rowden

SONIC**BOND**

sonicbondpublishing.com

Sonicbond Publishing Limited
www.sonicbondpublishing.co.uk
Email: info@sonicbondpublishing.co.uk

First Published in the United Kingdom 2021
First Published in the United States 2021

British Library Cataloguing in Publication Data:
A Catalogue record for this book is available from the British Library

Copyright Jez Rowden 2021

ISBN 978-1-78952-036-1

Typeset in ITC Garamond & ITC Avant Garde
Printed and bound in England

Graphic design and typesetting: Full Moon Media

Thanks to ...

A huge thank you is again due to Stephen Lambe and all at Sonicbond for allowing me to put this book together and dig deeper into the career of an artist I have admired for many years.

Aimee Mann has produced a string of idiosyncratic and highly engaging releases, each different to the last, exploring new sounds and textures to colour her songs, and what songs they are: always dripping with melody and filled with her wonderful words. She is truly a master of her craft and my deepest appreciation goes out to her.

I am also indebted to my wonderful wife Paula for her unstinting support and patience, allowing me to chip away at doing this when there were loads of other things that I should have been doing! Thank you so much Sweetheart, all my love. X

Would you like to write for Sonicbond Publishing?

We are mainly a music publisher, but we also occasionally publish in other genres including film and television. At Sonicbond Publishing we are always on the look-out for authors, particularly for our two main series, On Track and Decades.

Mixing fact with in depth analysis, the On Track series examines the entire recorded work of a particular musical artist or group. All genres are considered from easy listening and jazz to 60s soul to 90s pop, via rock and metal.

The Decades series singles out a particular decade in an artist or group's history and focuses on that decade in more detail than may be allowed in the On Track series.

While professional writing experience would, of course, be an advantage, the most important qualification is to have real enthusiasm and knowledge of your subject. First-time authors are welcomed, but the ability to write well in English is essential.

Sonicbond Publishing has distribution throughout Europe and North America, and all our books are also published in E-book form. Authors will be paid a royalty based on sales of their book. Further details about our books are available from www.sonicbondpublishing.com. To contact us, complete the contact form there or email info@sonicbondpublishing.co.uk

on track ...

Aimee Mann

Contents

Foreword

Let's face facts: Aimee Mann should be a damn sight more famous than she is, although I suspect that she quite likes things the way they are. For those familiar with her wonderful body of work, the two Grammy Awards, Oscar nomination and regular inclusion in lists of greatest living songwriters come as no surprise.

From her earliest days, with post-punk outfit The Young Snakes, through the 1980s chart hits and pop fame with 'Til Tuesday, right through a solo career of now nearly thirty years that has seen her fully embrace the singer-songwriter path, Aimee has crafted a song catalogue that is beyond reproach. Taking influence from Leonard Cohen, Stephen Sondheim and Jimmy Webb, among others, she has developed a style of her own, taking personal experience and the foibles of the human condition as a starting point for her vividly crafted songs.

What initially drew me to Aimee was her uncanny way with a melody, forging uncompromisingly upbeat hooks to cloak her dark tales of losers and misery. From her strikingly unexpected operatic falsetto with The Young Snakes and the epic pop of 'Til Tuesday, she made a deliberate move to a more comfortable style that works well in the intimate and personal spaces that her songs inhabit. Her warm and individualistic tones possess a charm and personality that cut through to speak to her listeners directly. It's understated, delicate, haunting and sweet in equal measure. She is also a particularly melodic and highly underrated bass player, an element she has largely moved away from over the years, acoustic guitar now being her instrument of choice.

Her songs possess a well-defined understanding of what makes great pop, finessing thoughts and tricky circumstances into beautifully arranged musical settings, always delivered in an effortlessly cool way. The message is often bleakly ironic, the brightness of the melodies delivering poignant vignettes as almost clandestine, hiding the true extent of the heartbreak and darkness, to be discovered, as in my case, much later. Her observational, slightly detached style looks at the underbelly of the relationships we form, showing her deep fascination with what makes us tick as an emotional species. She plays with language in intriguing ways, twisting scenarios and perspectives, often singing from the viewpoint of another and frequently directing her ire at her own choices: As she told the *LA Times* in 1993: 'I've certainly given other people the short end of the stick more times than I can count, and those are the times that I'm least proud of'.

Aimee has explained the origins and meanings of many of her songs, but some remain elusive. I have tried to interpret them in the way they come across to me – only Aimee knows for sure. My reasoning may not always work for you, or it may seem well off the mark, and that's fine. They're a personal perspective and not set in stone, best used as a starting point to discover how the songs work best for you. Her albums are a treasure trove of beautiful yet fierce words with the grit to keep listeners coming back for more, the process of writing this book opening them up still further for me. My hope is that both new listeners and existing fans can use it as a companion to the music, to listen that little bit closer to her beautiful songs. You won't be disappointed..

Beginnings

Aimee Elizabeth Mann was born on 8 September 1960 in Richmond, Virginia, growing up with an older brother, in the suburb of Bon Air. Her father was a painter and her mother a psychiatrist. They divorced when Aimee was three, her mother spiriting her away to London for nine months before her father managed to bring her back. She remained devoted to her father but did not see her mother again until she was an adult.

'I was always a tomboy who was pretty solitary, interested in reading and painting,' she told the *LA Times* in 1996. 'I was into all the stuff my father was interested in. We're very much alike. We like watching football games and eating asparagus.' Her childhood was not especially musical, although her father played piano. She took lessons from the age of six, but 'hated it because I just didn't get it'.

The first music that grabbed her attention was Peter, Paul & Mary. Her stepmother enjoyed Glen Campbell, which introduced her to the songs of Jimmy Webb, but as she confirmed to *Pennyblack Music* in 2017, the first album she bought was Elton John's *Madman Across the Water* because she liked the cover. 'I had no idea who he was. And then I took it home and I was like "Whaaaat?" ... it had a real melancholy, kind of spooky sound almost, that wasn't like other stuff that was out there. And I really liked it.'

Developing an interest in the performing arts, she joined her high school drama club, a teacher remembering her in an article in *Richmond's Style Weekly* in 2000, as 'a kid who had her own mind... She was a kind of an insecure kid, very quiet, very introspective ... I liked her a lot. When she did start talking, she was worth listening to'.

She discovered David Bowie and Bruce Springsteen, moving on to John Lydon and the Sex Pistols when punk broke. Her tastes took in arch outsiders like Devo and Talking Heads, but also the easier sounds of Frank Sinatra, Burt Bacharach and The Carpenters. However, she hated hard rock. She picked up a few guitar chords and learned to play Bob Dylan and Neil Young covers, but soon became intrigued by the bass guitar. Her family initially ridiculed her aspirations: 'They thought it was hilarious ...,' she said in an interview with the *LA Times* in 1985, 'I started saving money to buy a bass. My family laughed at me, so I gave up the idea for a long time. If I had started playing bass when I was 12 like I wanted to, I'd be an incredible bass player now'. Eventually, while working as a waitress in Richmond's *Holiday Inn*, she hung out with touring bands and learned rudimentary bass from a musician she got to know. He told her about Berklee College in Boston, and she discovered that you didn't have to audition for the seven-week summer schools they ran. She hadn't tried songwriting and knew no musical theory, but with an 'overwhelming urge to get out of town', she decided to follow her interest in music. Persuading her father to fund the course, she moved to Boston in 1978: 'The best thing that anyone can ever do – and that I certainly did – is make a choice not to be afraid anymore. I was a very fearful person,' she told *Billboard* in a 1993 article, 'and leaving Richmond to go to the big city of Boston by myself for music school when I knew nothing but four Neil Young chords on an acoustic guitar – that completely changed my life'.

Of her integration into musical education, in her 1995 artist biography for the Geffen label, she said, 'Once I got the underlying structure down, music stopped being this huge mystery. I became more interested and much better at it'. She was accepted on a vocals course at Berklee for the following academic year, but she 'quickly realised that no-one could teach me how to sing' and lessons didn't improve her vocals. Rather, she found that the repetition of songs was the key. She switched to bass: 'I didn't want to become a bass player necessarily – I wanted to learn how to read music'.

She worked hard and learnt bass and theory from the basics. Not knowing if she had any talent, learning was the key to finding out. She later noted that understanding theory was a key moment, changing music into something she could develop skills in. She connected with music but wasn't sure what her part in it might be. Fame didn't come into the equation; she just wanted to be a musician.

At this point, she knew little about technique but her desire to play drew her to the burgeoning punk scene, later commenting that she owed much to punk, as without the inclusiveness of the scene and the support from those involved, where you could do what you liked without having to be a great player, she would never have become a musician.

In a 2017 interview with *The Observer* she spoke of attending Berklee 'for four semesters and then I was concerned about wasting my father's money. So I dropped out. I had also started a band and I wanted to see what being a working band and playing shows was like'. It was 1981 and that band was The Young Snakes, 'a little punk, noise-art outfit', comprising Aimee on bass and vocals, with drummer Dave Brown and guitarist Doug Vargas. Dave came up with the name. They didn't like it, but it ended up sticking as they had bookings. Vargas was an angular player, heavily influenced by King Crimson's Robert Fripp. Aimee tried to sound like Nina Hagen and sang in a faux-operatic style: 'The idea of mixing punk with operatic singing, I thought, was amazing', she told the *Boston Globe* in 1993. There was an experimental edge – 'no matter how ridiculous', Aimee describing The Young Snakes as 'a bunch of noise', their music having 'weirdness upon weirdness'. They released *Bark Along with the Young Snakes* in 1982 (discussed in the Appendices of this book). 'We were deluding ourselves', she said in another interview with *The Globe* in 1985.

Whilst working at *Newbury Comics* in Boston, she concluded that being less experimental and more restrictive in the writing would be a better way forward in terms of value and interest. This more structured approach was tried with the Snakes towards the end of their run, but new wave and Roxy Music were becoming an influence and Aimee's dalliance with art-punk soon ended. Talking to the *LA Times* in 1985, she said: 'I realised I wanted to write about things that were important to me, that were happening in my life. I'm a romantic. I think a lot about love. I like to write haunting love songs with pretty melodies. If people think I'm one-dimensional and plastic because of that, I don't care. I could write love songs forever.'

In 2017, Aimee considered her decision to become a musician in an interview with *Guitar World*:

I didn't really have an innate ability to play by ear the way other people could, but I knew I wanted to learn about it. So I set a goal for myself. I'd go to school and learn about music until I hit a wall. I was always encouraged by getting better, writing songs and learning how to play. I started a band and when that one collapsed, I started another band. I never did hit that wall. But I also never thought about being a big star. I just said I'm going to go until I can't go anymore. It's the way I still feel about my career. I'm just going to keep going forward until I can't go forward anymore.

'Til Tuesday

After the Young Snakes collapsed, Aimee spent a short period as a member of an early iteration of Ministry (during their synth-pop period), while briefly dating band leader Al Jourgensen. Aimee and drummer Michael Hausman, a classmate from Berklee, became a couple, and after meeting English guitarist, Robert Holmes at a party, they were later introduced to Bronx-born keyboard player Joey Pesce, another Berklee alumnus. The quartet quickly hit it off and started playing regular gigs.

It has been suggested that the band's name (originally styled as 'til Tuesday) was taken from David Bowie's 'Love You 'til Tuesday' from 1967, or that as they rehearsed on that day each week, sessions would end with a cheery "Til Tuesday!". But in 1984, Aimee revealed to the *Boston Globe* that 'It was just something that finally sounded alright after hours and hours of stupid suggestions. We liked using a day of the week. We wanted a little phrase; we considered Sunday Best, that kind of thing'.

Taking it seriously from the start, they worked 'disposable' jobs whilst trying to make it as a band. Holmes was a few years older, and after a decade in bands, had more experience. His family had emigrated when he was seven, settling in Boston. The rest of the band were also from out of town and only in Boston to study. While the others came from punk and new wave backgrounds, Holmes was steeped in classic rock, developing a lovely echo-laden guitar technique, textural and quite minimalistic, that suited 'Til Tuesday, effectively filling spaces in the arrangements.

Aimee saw 'Til Tuesday as a rebellion against the 'no melody, no chord progression, no sweetness' of The Young Snakes, realising (as noted in her Geffen biography) that 'Not following the rules was a rule in itself and more limiting than anything else'. There was great confidence, as she stated to *The Boston Globe* in 1984, 'I know this band is going to be successful. It's not like I'm fooling myself – there's a definite place for us. There's a need for us. It may be a small one, but we're different enough, and we're the same enough. We thought it all out. We know what we're doing'. Of their sound, Aimee told *The Globe* in 1983 'I think it has enough of an edge, but I'm really a sucker for lush melodies and minor chords – melodies that are beautiful without being sappy'.

With Aimee the striking focal point, the others played their part in delivering a group image. Holmes' interesting androgynous look complemented the clean-cut Hausman, Pesce cutting a fine figure with his contemporary haircuts and dance moves. Holmes wryly observed to *The Boston Globe* in 1985, 'I think we're pretty much a democracy. We're four parts, but with Aimee as a tiebreaker'.

They recorded a demo, 'Love in a Vacuum', which got local airplay. *The Boston Globe* noted that they 'made an impressive mark with their cool, airy brand of white funk … equally oriented toward rhythmic grooves and melodic hooks' with lyrics 'often about tense, difficult relationships'. With their audience increasing, they won WBCN's *Rock & Roll Rumble* in 1983 with its $2,000 prize.

The daughter of an executive at Epic Records heard 'Til Tuesday on the radio and convinced him to check them out. Seven months after forming, they were signed to Epic by A&R man, Dick Wingate, Joey Pesce telling *Spin* in 1986 that Epic 'seemed the most down-to-earth and didn't want Aimee in leather and have her swallow the microphone'. Aimee was quick to credit the vibrant Boston music scene and the support of local radio in the band's success.

They had proven themselves a great live act and successfully developed a collection of songs that set them apart. Early material from before the debut album shows more funk and a punk edge to their new wave sound, successfully smoothed off for mass-market appeal once a major label became involved. The band seemed to be having more fun at this stage, doing their own thing before it became a business in the public eye. A concert at *The Spit* in Boston on 1 March 1984, broadcast at the time on WFNX, was unofficially released as *Voices Carry – Live* in 2015. Not all the fifteen tracks were ever officially released, the quality is very poor (with vocals crazily low in the mix for the first half), but it gives an idea of what a sharp live band they were at that time.

The recording of the debut album was a new experience for them and something of a blur. Released in 1985, the title song from *Voices Carry* became a big US hit, helped by the powerful video which received much airtime on the fledgeling *MTV*, already an important factor in breaking new chart music. 'Til Tuesday went on to win that year's *MTV* Video Music Award for Best New Artist. The video's success and its iconic image statement turned out to be difficult to escape.

Hall & Oates' guitarist, G. E. Smith, showed the video to Daryl Hall, whose representative called 'Til Tuesday – during the album release party – to offer them a tour support slot. Within days they found themselves playing nationwide arena shows to audiences of 20,000.

With her appealing image, helped by a great song getting heavy rotation, Aimee proved to be a huge draw, and she got her 'brush-up with fame, when 'Til Tuesday was popular for a minute'. The initial success seemed to please her. She told the *LA Times* in 1985: 'You can now be in the music business and not get into that ridiculous, sleazy lifestyle where you're always drunk or stoned or coked-out or you're sleeping your way to the top. You can be popular without being a degenerate'. However, she found people following her home very strange and not at all to her liking, noting that 'Your recognisability exceeds your success'. Travelling in a van, staying in cheap motels and earning $150 a week, they were 'kind of famous' but completely broke: 'I judged that I'd made it when I could afford to buy contact lens solution whenever I needed it!'. The assumption was that she had made it big, but forging a career has always been fraught with difficulty, and she continues to stress the realities, telling *The Observer* in 2017: 'I don't think people understand how hard it is to even make a living'.

Her drive to make a success of a singing and writing career led Aimee – in spite of timid beginnings – to throw herself fully into band performance and promotion. But after the initial rush, the realisation dawned that her life was no longer her own. Although things died down after a couple of years, she became wary of the media spotlight: 'It was very difficult to deal with that' she told *Style Weekly* in 2000, 'it takes a certain kind of person to enjoy being stared at 24 hours a day. I find it more intrusive than enjoyable'. In 2017 she told *Billboard*, 'Only a real narcissist enjoys constant attention. To me, constant attention feels vaguely threatening. People expect things out of you you're not going to be able to deliver … if we're going into the hotel and somebody offers to carry my suitcase or something, it's like "Oh, they're being really nice because they're my friend". You can't pretend to yourself that you as a person are so wonderful that people just want to carry your bags all the time! It's not like people carry my bags, but still…'.

The second 'Til Tuesday album, 1986's *Welcome Home*, was softer and more acoustic, leading to arguments with Epic about direction. Nothing really took off and Joey Pesce quit, replaced by Michael Montes.

Throughout their recording career, the band evolved significantly as Aimee's songwriting developed. 'Til Tuesday 'were sort of doing, like, post-new-wave dance-pop stuff' she told *Stereogum* in 2018, 'I started to feel like it was not really my thing. Acoustic guitar music was what I was more influenced by and what came naturally to me'. This direction became more apparent by the band's third and final album, 1988's *Everything's Different Now*. Holmes and Montes left after the recording but before the album appeared. Now effectively a duo, Aimee and Michael Hausman toured in support with session musicians, but with no record company promotion, it did nothing sales-wise. The band's recording career effectively came to an end a month after the album's release when Epic stated that no further band recordings would be sanctioned, although they wanted to keep Aimee under contract to work with outside writers like Dianne Warren and Desmond Child. This arrangement did not appeal to Aimee, as she told *The Independent* in 1995: 'Their songs say nothing, they have no real personal viewpoint, there's no cleverness, no truthfulness'. Of the label's quest for fame, she said 'I nearly had a heart attack. I thought: "I can't do it. I'm not capable of being a big star". I said, "Look, don't put me in an arena and expect me to make my gestures large, where everything has to be amazing, perfect and fabulous. I'm tired of fabulous. I can be a really good songwriter, but I can't be fabulous. It's not going to happen. My gestures are small!". She is not a fan of 'that grand-gesture-type songwriting, those glorious topics with huge references, where you say how you feel about something instead of showing the reality of the situation and thus describing your feelings... well, they're a model for me of how not to write songs … You can only write a completely universal song by making it truly personal'.

The bitter dispute between artist and label damaged an already sour relationship. Aimee told Epic that as they didn't like what she did, they should go their separate ways, describing their response to the BBC in 1995 as 'No, we love what you're doing, as long as it's completely different from what you're doing, we will love it' … and the message was really clear, the label commented 'We're going to kill your records until you do this, and we're not going to release you because we know you'd like to go'. She had seven more records to make for them, so she was potentially in forever.

Mann and Hausman continued to tour under the 'Til Tuesday banner until 1990. Aimee then embarked on her solo career which, after legal hassles to extricate herself from her contract, officially began in 1992.

Voices Carry (1985)

Personnel:
Aimee Mann: Vocals, Bass Guitar
Robert Holmes: Guitars, Background Vocals
Joey Pesce: Piano, Synthesisers, Background Vocals
Michael Hausman: Drums and Percussion
Producer: Mike Thorne
Released: 20 April 1985
Record Label: Epic
Recorded: R.P.M. Sound Studios
Running Time: 41:52
Highest chart place: US:19, UK: -

Martin Rushent, who had made his name with post-punk, new wave and synth-pop artists, was initially considered as producer, before Mike Thorne – another Englishman with a similar background – was eventually hired. Thorne had produced Soft Cell's 'Tainted Love' and Bronski Beat's 'Smalltown Boy' singles and had a good ear for a hit.

By Thorne's account in *Stereo Society* in 1999, the sessions in New York were 'pleasant and relatively uneventful'. The band were not only competent musicians with distinctive instrumental voices, they were also flexible and able to spot interesting musical directions when they appeared. Thorne noted Aimee to be an 'articulate, tough-minded extrovert; the other three were slower to confrontation but just as sharp'. They had come together at the right time and forged a sound that fit well with current trends. Coupled with a batch of quality songs, this led to immediate success, Mann's lyrics framed in music co-written by the whole band.

Voices Carry was released in April 1985, preceded by the title track in March, 'Til Tuesday's emergence catching the record-buying public unaware. Thorne saw the band as 'passionate, entertaining, intelligent and stylish', fronted by Aimee, her peroxide hair with thin braid becoming an important visual cue that factored well with the fashions of the time, accentuated in band images and on record sleeve. The advent of *MTV* had made video a key factor in a song's success, and in 'Voices Carry' they had a striking example to help spread the word.

The *Los Angeles Times* called Aimee 'a star in the making – her vocals have a girl's innocence and a woman's sophistication, with a tangible ache lurking just beneath [her] tense yet cool surface', also noting that 'she's got the best cheekbones since Sting'. *Spin* reported the album as 'a pleasure, but not a revelation', noting Aimee's look and 'a voice that's evocative, though not yet distinctive enough to stake out its own turf in the crowded field of female vocalists'. Robert Christgau likened the synth-pop hooks to A Flock of Seagulls, Mann providing a more human face. However, the 'recognisable romantic cliché' of the 'aggressively banal lyrics' pointed towards product rather than artistic expression. In a recent retrospective, *AllMusic* praised Mann's lyrics as setting 'Til Tuesday apart from the raft of similar bands plying their trade in the mid-1980s, noting that they should have achieved greater success with subsequent albums.

Listening to *Voices Carry* today, it's a fine collection, certainly flavoured with sound choices that place it squarely in the 1980s, but (with a couple of exceptions) not overly dated and the songs speak for themselves. It's bright and upbeat, forged from quality pop sensibilities. The playing is good with a keen ensemble feel, Michael's drums keeping things steady, nothing flashy, while Joey's keyboards are generally more interesting than the standard fare. Aimee's bass is a key focus, playing lead on some songs with a defined groove in her slap technique, but the star of the show is often Robert's understated and echo-laden guitar, giving the songs depth as he steps forward with vital contributions. Vocally, the album is far removed from the career that Aimee would eventually carve out for herself. She sings well, if a little thin at times, such widescreen pop crying out for a more powerful voice to get the hairs on the neck standing to attention. Nevertheless, it's a confident performance that successfully delivers the songs. And what songs they are, at least four classics with a fine supporting cast.

The album went gold in the US and Canada but there was a sting in the tail for Thorne when a friend commented on how bad it sounded. This surprised him. He had enjoyed the experience and was happy with the results. His friend's copy sounded 'screechy, low in level, completely lacking the power of the original'. An investigation by Epic revealed that the album had been 're-cut at the pressing plant' by 'the night shift' in response to the high demand. Despite this revelation, sub-standard copies continued to appear in later pressings, much to Thorne's chagrin.

'Love In A Vacuum' ('Til Tuesday, Lyrics: Mann) (3:34)

From the slap bass intro, this is a 1980s classic. Mike Thorne confirmed that the arrangement changed from 'a fairly laid back piece launched by Joey's synthesiser bass line to an aggressive, catchy song when, following my suggestion and much practice of the resulting difficult part by her, Aimee's bass had appropriated his figure for the recording'. A wise move – the demo version (and *Voices Carry – Live* performance) with synth intro sounds very dated now.

The harmonies and staccato guitar immediately provide drive and energy, Aimee's voice having a ballsy edge. The sound expands into the chorus, sweeping synths, a picked-out keyboard line and twangy bass keeping things moving. With a synth counter-melody carrying into the bridge, Aimee sings almost alone before soaring again. Her voice carries some interesting phrasing and tonality if maybe a little shrill at times – a very different instrument from what it would become.

Lyrically, it describes the bubble of a relationship where initial feelings can decay, selfishness and possessive thoughts creeping in to replace the carefree early days. Ultimately, the loneliness of obsession leads to an almost inevitable split: 'I look in your eyes, I realise what you've sold me, You say it's me, But I know that it isn't'.

Relegated from its initial first choice position to become the third single, released in November 1985, it failed to chart. The video begins in black and white, Aimee play-fighting with a boyfriend. Things seem good; he hangs her picture on the wall, but he soon becomes distant and controlling, the picture a metaphor for the prison she now finds herself in. The band appear to play the chorus in colour before the scene resumes. It deviates from the lyric as the couple appear reunited by the end, no doubt a marketing ploy to keep things positive. Aimee had to fight the directors to prevent them slavishly copying scenes from Jean-Luc Godard's *Breathless.*

The remix agreement in Mike Thorne's contract was overridden for the first two singles, which were handled by Bob Clearmountain. Here, Thorne and Harvey Goldberg made 7" and extended 12" versions that 'we felt were among our personal best work. The 7" was powerful, and the 12" had an extraordinary combination of dance power and rock and roll sheen. Using early samplers, I added short sections from the previous two singles over the top of the new rhythm track, forming a novel piece verging on being a latter-day 'Til Tuesday medley'. After delivery to Epic, nothing more was heard. Upon release, the 7" had been remixed and, in Mike's words, was 'an unmitigated disaster. Aimee's heroic opening bass lick was edited to the point of butchery, and the sound was badly defined and muddy... one of the brightest and most spectacular new group starts of the year had been shattered by incompetence and arrogance'.

'Looking Over My Shoulder' ('Til Tuesday, Lyrics: Mann) (4:15)

Remixed by Bob Clearmountain as the second single in August 1985, it reached only 61 in the *Billboard Hot 100*. The bass is still front and centre with a funky slapping edge; the melody carried on guitar. Aimee sings low, showing the range at her disposal, picking up into the gorgeous rising chorus. Keyboards float around the main melodies, coming to the fore at the end, working with the vocal over the steady rhythm. It is already apparent how adept 'Til Tuesday were at integrating melodic hooks into fully realised pop songs.

Lyrically, it's about unrequited infatuation, almost to the point of obsession, with the underlying awareness that it will end in disappointment 'because I know I haven't a prayer'. The video shows the band members watching the 'Voices Carry' promo on TV. An argument ensues about Aimee's role as the focal point, Robert pointing out 'We're supposed to be a band!'. Aimee imagines herself in a white ballgown, descending a circular staircase, the centre of attention, but the guys lurk in the shadows, lunging out to startle her. She pushes them away, but they are always nearby and she becomes more distraught. In the classic tradition, she wakes to find it was just a dream and they're all still friends, but on the screen in her white dress, Aimee sits weeping. It certainly plays with the band's image but is probably a bit too close for comfort.

'I Could Get Used To This' ('Til Tuesday, Lyrics: Mann) (3:02)
Unlike the first two songs, this one has not aged as well, its sound dating it
as squarely in the early 1980s, particularly the guitar and funky bass intro.
Unsurprising, but the true classics from *Voices Carry* still stand out. That said,
AllMusic highlighted the haunting lyric that helped to distance them from
similar bands of the time.

The words are sophisticated in structure and delivery. It seems positive – 'So
far … So good, I could get used to feeling the way that I do'. She doesn't want
to keep the relationship a secret, but there's the usual sting as 'Love is just too
difficult … I'm only talking to myself about it, So sad, I guess I'm going to have
to live without … I know how it goes'. However, there's questioning hope near
the end with 'Baby, will I get the chance?'.

The pace is steadier, Mann strutting through the vocal with confidence and,
ultimately, it's very engaging, popping bass bouncing along with various synth
tones, guitar doubled in a supporting role.

'No More Crying' ('Til Tuesday, Lyrics: Mann) (4:18)
The words here are particularly damning:

> There is no love here
> Only some sort of blackmail
>
> Found myself thinking
> He was almost sincere
> But you know rumours
> You believe what you hear
>
> I saw it coming
> It's the same old story
> You ignore his lying
> Believe him when he says that he's sorry
> No more crying over you…

Ouch! But who caused all this anger? In his 2013 autobiography, Al Jourgensen
spoke of his brief romance with Aimee. Jourgensen claimed that he was
the inspiration for 'Voices Carry'. However, speaking to *MTV*, he could not
remember the name of the song and admitted that he had never heard it or
seen the video. Mann stated to *Rolling Stone* in 1985 that 'No More Crying'
was about Al and 'nothing else'. Jourgensen spoke of their 'dysfunctional
relationship', saying that he had seen Aimee recently and they still got along.
He took it as a good sign, saying to himself, 'OK, you were an asshole at times,
but you weren't a complete asshole all the time'.

Bass leading the way, it kicks off when the repeated four-note guitar
figure comes in for the simple but effective chorus. There's a sparseness that

allows room for Mann to work the melody, selling the song and hitting some particularly high notes. Synth details shine after the breakdown, the textures fitting the sophisticated feel, suitably dark in the verses but lighter for the chorus.

'Voices Carry' ('Til Tuesday, Lyrics: Mann) (4:19)

The first 'Til Tuesday release and a major success, reaching number eight on *Billboard*, and also the Top 20 in Australia and Canada. Originally passed over for first single, it was A&R man Dick Wingate's shrewd choice to release it in a reworded form that seemed to precisely define the band and its style. The 7" featured a 3:59 Bob Clearmountain edited remix. Speaking to *Musician* in 1993, Aimee said, 'We never thought of it as a real pop song'.

AllMusic stated, 'One of the most distinctive radio singles of its era', also noting how Mann's breathy voice and the chorus brilliantly release the tension that builds throughout its 'stark, paranoid verses'. Said to have been inspired by an argument between her and Hausman after they broke off their relationship before the album's release, it was actually one of Aimee's earliest songs, the original lyric sung from the male perspective, the words based on a skittish girlfriend. Early recordings are available of the band playing it in its original form. Given perceptions at the time, Epic was concerned that the powerful mainstream commerciality of the song might be damaged by the perceived 'gay vibe', so they insisted that the lyric be altered to change the gender of the love interest. Thus the premise of a relationship deemed controversial moved to one of domestic abuse and control, although you can still hear the alternative meaning in the words.

Cyndi Lauper wanted to record 'Voices Carry' with the original lyric as the follow-up to her huge hit 'Girls Just Want to Have Fun', but only if the band left it off their release. Sensing the wide appeal, 'Til Tuesday kept it for themselves.

There's a swagger to the guitar and synths, Mann's voice at first edgy, gaining confidence into the chorus as she's warned that raised voices could be heard by the neighbours. Aimee's delivery brings the fear and control into focus, rising towards the conclusion, giving it all she's got. There's a natural fragility to her voice that works well here, backed up with real power and conviction.

The video was pivotal to the song's success, Mann's no-nonsense image making her something of a feminist icon. It became an *MTV* favourite, a well-realised and memorable piece which resonated with audiences. The oppressive and well-to-do boyfriend (played by Cully Holland) tries to get musician Aimee to quit her band and change her look by coercive means to fit in with his upper-class lifestyle. He wants her to be someone she isn't, but she eventually fights back whilst attending the opera with him at New York's *Carnegie Hall*.

Except for a short establishing shot of *Carnegie Hall*'s exterior, the video was filmed entirely in Boston, at an apartment on Brookline Street, and at the Strand Theater for the final interiors where Mann rises from her seat to belt out 'He said, shut up, He said, shut up, Oh God, can't you keep it down' while removing her cap to reveal her signature spiky hair. Her mortified boyfriend cringes in the next seat as other concert-goers look on aghast. According to Mann, it was director DJ Webster's idea to add this scene, inspired by Alfred Hitchcock's *The Man Who Knew Too Much,* Doris Day screaming during a symphony to thwart a murder. As for the acting, Aimee based her performance on real-life experiences: 'Yeah, I remember this, Grrr... and it's there'. A snowstorm had deterred potential extras from attending for the dramatic final scene, so to avoid showing empty seats, the camera couldn't pull back as far as was planned.

'Winning The War' ('Til Tuesday, Lyrics: Mann) (4:03)

Coming in like Duran Duran, it soon settles into a popping bassline, akin to 'Love in a Vacuum', with excellent guitar from Holmes. The keys are effective, tastefully filling the space and adding new lines. A minute in, Aimee begins to sing, possibly lacking the power at the top of her range to carry it off, but the song itself works well, conjuring images of crowded 1980s dancefloors.

Despite the long instrumental intro, it's musically light. Lyrically, it's another troubled relationship, a couple at each other's throats, the protagonist noting that 'You fight just for the sake of it, You know what hurts the most'. The constant battles threaten to 'close the door on happy ever after' and there's irony in 'We should have stopped it long ago, When there was love still'. It's a bleak representation of a romance that is past its sell-by date. The words are quite repetitive, but it's a toe-tapper that successfully keeps the momentum.

'You Know The Rest' ('Til Tuesday, Lyrics: Mann) (4:26)

This sedate ballad comes in beautifully on a keyboard line with chorded support. Stripped back, Aimee's voice is the melodic highpoint, rising majestically into the chorus, supported by Joey. She puts in a great performance here, particularly the wordless phrases before the second chorus. Piano is used to good effect and it's a fine song, one of the best on *Voices Carry*, culminating in an expansive finish to the fade.

This one might have been inspired by Mann's failing relationship with Hausman; there's clearly a lot of affection left. It's a gentle song, with sadness in lines like 'When you trusted me that was just a guess', acknowledging failings on both sides, and there's an almost apologetic air in places with regret for something now lost:

> Well, I warned you once
> But without success
> And I just escape
> With my heart a mess

'Maybe Monday' ('Til Tuesday, Lyrics: Mann) (3:40)

The punchy full-band intro is a nice change of pace, Holmes adding lovely phrases as it pulls back before launching into the chorus, which is a winner, getting stronger as the song develops. Aimee is light and airy, heading towards the top of her range. Again, a more powerful voice may have served this quirky number better, but she does a fine job. Guitar and keyboards combine at the end with a nice new wave vibe.

The words suggest repeated promises that he never delivers, leaving her hanging on. There's an element of control here too, and if there's one thing Aimee isn't keen on, that's it. The verses are her side of a conversation, talking to herself in the chorus, and she appears to be coming to the conclusion that she's being taken for a mug:

> It makes me laugh
> I'm spending all my time
> Staring at his photograph
> And that's the catch
> Oh, I feel foolish
> But I know it's really all I have

The opening track on *Voices Carry – Live*, the sound quality is so poor that Aimee can barely be heard.

'Are You Serious?' ('Til Tuesday, Lyrics: Mann) (3:15)

Played live as early as 1983, it's another worthy intro from Holmes, slapped bass picking things up amid subtle keys. Aimee is as engaging as ever and the chorus is bright and fun, but it gets a little repetitive and is a bit lightweight compared to others in the set. There's good instrumental work after the second chorus, Holmes adding backing vocals and some dextrous playing before a nicely realised synth solo from Pesce.

To me, this one sees Aimee as the protagonist, chasing a man who isn't interested. She's been here before but hasn't learnt the lesson and seems incapable of listening to the signals he's sending. It's pretty brutal as he responds 'Are you serious?' in the chorus. The second verse is the clincher; she rings him, but he tells whoever answers to say he isn't home, which gets the response 'Are you afraid to see me crying, Or is it that you're just too used to lying?'. It's sharp and to the point, each party equally blunt.

'Don't Watch Me Bleed' ('Til Tuesday, Lyrics: Mann) (3:26)

Another song with verses about a dead relationship and a chorus repeated a time or two too many. There's been lying and controlling, but he's finally leaving:

> So don't just kiss me goodbye
> That's not what I need
> Don't just kiss me goodbye
> Don't watch me bleed

Guitar stalks in over a sparse beat, punctuated by keys. It's more new wave than others, with a straighter bass line, the finely crafted pop edge still present. There's more meat to the vocals, with close harmonies through to the anguished final line. The delivery is particularly mature, Holmes the star with an excellent solo, of which there aren't many on this record.

'Sleep' ('Til Tuesday, Lyrics: Mann) (3:40)

With chiming keys and an easy pace, Aimee sings over the sparsest of backings, Holmes picking things up before the chorus, which is nice without really grabbing the attention. There is a more orchestrated feel with excellent keyboard embellishments, the album finishing with those chiming keys and vocals.

It seems to be lamenting a death, possibly of a baby, the ominous repeated 'He is waiting' in the chorus referring to God, or the Reaper. It might be that a literal interpretation is well off the mark, but lines like 'Thought you'd live forever, Thought you'd never die' and 'Oh, when you get to heaven, Tell me what you find' seem to leave little ambiguity, a plaintive 'Peace of mind, I hope' suggesting a troubled soul.

It's a sad way to end, but strangely uplifting with the chiming harmony chorus fade.

Related Tracks

Other songs from the band's early days didn't make *Voices Carry*. Those that have found their way online are listed alphabetically below. They're of variable quality, but as a taster of early 'Til Tuesday, they are worth checking out. No doubt others exist.

'Always For You'

I've only found a 44-second fragment of this one. Bass-heavy with a sweet vocal, it promised much.

'Enough To Save You' (4:33)

This stayed in the live sets until 1986, although during a show from that time, Aimee refers to it as a 'new song'. It has pace and nice guitar from Holmes, Aimee sounding husky. It would have fit on either of the first two albums, maybe being dropped due to the different vocal style.

'Five Minutes More' (3:47)

A light ballad, unlike any of the other early songs. It's pretty with a nice chorus and good vocal harmonies, washes of synth carrying it along.

'I'll Wait For You' (aka 'Boy') (4:26)

A funk-pop number that would have made an album prior to *Voices Carry* sound very different but no less appealing. Included on *Voices Carry – Live*, the vocals are so low as to be almost inaudible, but it's an excellent strutting instrumental with slap bass, distinctive twinkling keys and excellent guitar from Holmes. It was still being played live in 1986.

'I'm Gonna Do My Best' (3:12)
Another from *Voices Carry – Live*, it fits well in the funky pop vein of the early material, but the echoing vocal effects in an already muddy mix are hideous, making it borderline unlistenable.

'Just Like Me' (2:56)
This song exists in pretty good demo form. It's lighter than some of the others but with a good hook and could have worked on *Voices Carry*, although it possibly missed the cut for being slightly underdeveloped. Aimee puts in a solid vocal with shards of ringing guitar from Holmes. Still being played live in 1986, by then, it's well bedded-in, synths filling out the sound in the second half.

'Just Three Words' (3:23)
Another funky and popping mid-tempo number that appeared in videos of early live shows and on *Voices Carry – Live*. There's smoothness from the keys but the staccato guitar probably meant it couldn't find a home on *Voices Carry*. It's a quality track with a strong chorus, a shame that it never appeared.

'Learning You By Heart' (3:31)
Played in 1983, often as set opener, it's up-tempo and pumping with slap bass. The music generally had a funkier aspect at this stage, but with cool synths that fitted the new wave sound.

'Love Or Money' (4:04)
Played as the encore of *Voices Carry – Live*, a brooding intro and theatrical vocal lead into a confident song, different from the album material, so no surprise that it didn't feature. A shame, though it has lots going for it.

'Opposites Attract' (3:10)
Aimee's performance is very strong in a driving piece with unorthodox guitar. The chorus is solid and the vocal harmonies work very well. Good stuff.

'Out Of The Question' (3:34)
More up-tempo funky pop with harmonics and quick-fire guitar from Holmes (showing what a fine stylist he is). The harmony vocals are good and like most of these early tracks, it's a fun live number.

'Tension' (4:16)
From *Voices Carry – Live*, in a familiar pattern, there's a funky pop edge, Aimee singing low with good support from Holmes and Pesce.

'Unknown Rift' (3:03)
A feature of early sets, this funky piece is included on *Voices Carry – Live* where the vocals are again almost inaudible. The instrumental side is excellent, strutting with slap bass building on Holmes' prodigious guitar work.

'You Just Can't Give It Up' (3:00)
Another from *Voices Carry – Live*, poppy with slap bass. It's a little light and throwaway, but a fun number.

'You Still Love Me From A Distance' (2:59)
More funky pop in the vein of their earliest material.

Welcome Home (1986)

Personnel:
Aimee Mann: Vocals, Bass Guitar
Joey Pesce: Piano, Synthesizers, Background Vocals
Robert Holmes: Guitars, Background Vocals
Michael Hausman: Drums & Percussion
Producer: Rhett Davies
Released: 15 June 1986
Record Label: Epic Records
Recorded: Bearsville Studios
Running Time: 40:31
Highest chart place: US:49, UK: –

Aimee settled into writing most of the songs on her own for what would prove to be a difficult follow-up to *Voices Carry*, resentment surfacing amongst band members. In 1989, looking back with *The Chicago Tribune*, she said, 'Everybody was really pleased with the second album, but when it was not successful, they were looking for someone to blame, I became the scapegoat.'

She wrote on acoustic guitar this time, away from the drum machines and synthesisers, giving the songs a folkier feel. This alteration to the band's sound concerned Epic, who demanded more consistency with the *Voices Carry* template. As she told *Musician* in 1993, 'I don't think Epic ever understood what I wanted to do'. However, Aimee was right to stick to her guns as *Welcome Home* is a much more mature collection, showing her development as a songwriter, and taking the band's sound outside the parameters set by the debut. This striving for artistic credibility in preference to chasing the money and coming up with *Voices Carry II* (which would have no doubt bolstered their place in the public's consciousness) shows that even at this early stage, Aimee remained true to herself, wanting to create music that she felt comfortable with whilst continually working at her craft. By now known for their sleek, high-tech style of new wave, the band gambled with the move to a less keyboard-driven, organic sound, influenced by Roxy Music's *Avalon*.

Again featuring the band alone with no outside contributions, it contains many wonderful and skilful songs and is a huge step up from the debut. *Welcome Home* was a creative triumph for 'Til Tuesday, deserving wider attention than it achieved. The critical reaction was positive, but lead single 'What About Love' could only manage number 26 in the US, and the album was a commercial disappointment, just scraping the Top 50.

Produced by Rhett Davies, Robert Holmes saw this album as something of an epiphany. She told *Sorbus Minima* in 2018: 'I began to grasp the standards that top professional people with serious ears had and I also realised that I wasn't at that level yet. I was flabbergasted by the attention to detail they paid and the whole experience was thrilling and highly educational'.

Again, Aimee's discomfort with fame and being a recognisable public figure was obvious. It wasn't about that for her. When later asked by *Rolling Stone* what became of her blond braid, she replied, 'I think it may be in a cigar box somewhere. What drove me to cut it off was that backstage at a show, some fan wanted to get a picture taken with me, and they said, "Hold up the braid!". I said, "That's the last fuckin' straw"'.

Welcome Home has aged very well. The band are bedded-in and the songs show development in writing and sound choices. The playing is again first-rate, the feel much less that of a pop album with an increasingly sophisticated appeal.

'What About Love' (Mann) (3:56)

The opener follows on from *Voices Carry* with a sound heavy with that 1980s feel, particularly in the drums, which tend to plod a little. Aimee is in fine voice, resonant and smoky in her lower registers, and the chorus is a winner, opening up as the hook hits. Holmes adds shards of piercing guitar, with a soaring yet slightly mournful solo that fits the mood. The synth pops are a fun embellishment, but they do add to the dated feel.

There's a yearning quality, a relationship going nowhere, the singer pleading for more space for love as real-life grinds away, her partner's work perhaps leaving little time. She's 'Living in silence, Living by the book' and 'Getting pretty tired of living on hope'. Throughout the song, the 'What about you?' lines are directed at the absent partner, until the final plaintive 'What about me?'.

Just scraping the Top 30 was a disappointment and it deserved better. An extended mix was included in the single package, pushing the running time to six-and-a-half minutes with an elongated instrumental intro, a run-through of the chorus before the first verse, and a stripped-back instrumental section led by the bass at around four minutes. An interesting and worthy mix.

The video starts with a couple (featuring Aimee) enjoying a steamy tussle in the shadows. She wakes alone in bed, the scene cutting to a café where she sits with Michael Hausman. The guy she was kissing at the start is seated at the next table. The mid-section sees the band playing, then Aimee and her new lover appear in a rowing boat before canoodling in the great outdoors.

'Coming Up Close' (Mann) (4:40)

A clean guitar phrase bookends the low-key first verse, the chorus exploding after the second on a soaring, easy hook supported by piano. With key lines harmonised, there's a folky feel, the uplifting and Abba-esque tones holding an underlying sadness, intimate words painting a beautiful picture. Aimee's vocal is spot on, the strange cadence of the last two lines of the chorus effortlessly accommodating the words and adding to the unusually vivid nature of the song, which ends with Aimee's elongated cry of 'Come on home!'.

Aimee confided that this was one of her most autobiographical early songs. There's a 'young love' feel, but it could describe a more recent experience from touring the first album, life on the road and the loneliness that can bring. A couple in a borrowed car listen to Bob Dylan as they drive the roads of rural Iowa. It's a gorgeous summer night with 'promises in every star'. The line 'I felt my heartbeat back a weekend's worth of sadness' is simply sublime. The second verse takes things further as they find a deserted farmhouse and carve their names, dreams of a life together 'coming up close' with a sense of everything falling into place. An epiphany in the wordless connection gives a warm and welcoming vision of the house rebuilt, home for a life together. Ultimately, it isn't meant to be; he drops her back at her hotel and drives away, a strange situation after what appeared to be a perfect evening, showing that in their hearts they both know that the future they imagined could never be. The evocative words are filled with detail, conjuring beautiful images. Maybe in hindsight, she realises that it was more perfect than she thought, and they could have made it work.

Clearly considered a key song, words from the chorus provided the album's title, and as second single it barely broke into the Top 60 in early 1987. The video features the band playing the song live, Aimee on acoustic guitar, with no additional imagery.

'On Sunday' (Hausman, Holmes, Mann, Pesce) (4:06)

The jaunty opening punch rides a solid rhythm with chorded guitar and interesting synth textures. The vocal slides quickly into a pre-chorus before the full power lands, and what a chorus it is, Aimee heading towards the heights. Holmes solos briefly before the second verse, the instrumental bridge paring things back, building again for the final chorus in a nice variation that enhances the power. Ending on an elegant descending chord pattern, it's a brilliant song delivered to perfection, the album's first whole-band co-write showing the confidence they now had in writing ensemble pieces to showcase the unit's full force.

There's a strange dichotomy in the lyric; is she saying that he should just take his misery elsewhere and leave her alone, or does she wait for him to come to her so they can be happy? The chorus of 'So why spend your sadness now, Save it up for me, And why is lonely all you have, When love is what you'll find on Sunday', initially suggests that he saves his misery to share with her when they meet. However, the second part is more positive; why is he alone when together they can be in love? A lot depends on interpretation, but the second verse is sneeringly cynical:

You might guard your heart
But it's awfully fun to have it broken
Or at least to leave a bruise
It becomes an art
Though the rules of which are rarely spoken
By the lucky ones who can choose

This suggests a necessity to toughen up and guard yourself after numerous heartaches. Love is a game for some: they're the ones who decide the rules while their victims collect mementoes of the inflicted pain, building each time until the 'souvenirs become your world'.

It could be that the singer is talking about herself, hanging on a string, miserable until he makes time for her, Sunday delineated as the only day they can be together. It's breathtakingly well put together with an intriguing heart, Aimee again showing her talent for writing words that resonate.

'Will She Just Fall Down' (Mann) (2:49)

The strutting keyboard intro is great, a walking bassline carrying through this short and punchy number. Low register vocals set the scene before the chorus, Holmes producing telling chords. But the synth textures hold sway, colouring this upbeat song that gives the album a different spin. An unusual piece that underlines the quality of *Welcome Home*.

But what is it about? There is a lot to consider and no direct path. It sounds like concern for a friend's well-being. She seems to be walking her own path through life and trying to resolve things for herself. But do the 'two unmatched gloves' suggest someone not taking care of detail, as perhaps the result of too much to drink? Does she need support in an emotional sense, or is it more literal? She seems to have a problem which she needs to work out alone, but will that solitude push her over the edge? There's a sadness which she seems unable to display in public, keeping it to herself and drowning in misery when alone. It would help to talk, but she can't, the jauntiness of the music masking the dilemma of the words and how to help this friend in need.

It could be sung from the perspective of a partner in a relationship, the third verse cryptically suggesting a gifted watch as a metaphor for keeping her, perhaps mentally, on the right path. The 'watch' helps to guide her, but she needs help to remember to keep it wound and working:

And on her birthday I'll
Get a watch to keep her time
And I'll stay up with her
When she forgets to wind it

'David Denies' (Hausman, Holmes, Mann, Pesce) (4:50)

The strident opening is reined back for the first verse, driven by piano and delivered with a sense of innocence. The divine chorus floods in after the second verse, bombastic with soaring guitars and walls of keyboards, another example of the whole group contributing to the writing. The instrumental section is straightforward but effective, resetting the tone before a reiteration of the chorus. Finally, the lines 'And so I'll wait and so I'll hope, Somehow I can convince him not to let me go' are delivered forcefully as a final gesture of hope.

It appears that David is married, promising to leave his wife and be with the singer, but he never does. He denies changing his mind, but the singer knows that he always will. Despite this, she continues to hope that one day she can persuade him to stay with her. The use of 'Its what he wants I'm almost sure' is telling, as if she's trying to convince herself while he continues to toy with her emotions. In the meantime, all three of them are miserable, a situation which requires an outcome.

'Lovers' Day' (Mann, Pesce) (4:19)
A rare Mann/Pesce co-write, the faded intro leading into a dated keyboard-heavy sound. Holmes' guitars fragment beautifully with occasional melody lines, the vocal delivery reminiscent of Aimee's later solo work. Robert gets to solo elegantly towards the end with Aimee emoting 'There's no such thing as Lovers' Day'.

The confident drive masks a darker edge that leaves it at odds with much of the rest of the album, maybe hinting at what a follow-up to *Voices Carry* would have sounded like if they'd followed a more direct path. The chorus has a distinctly new wave edge with a hint of Goth, the underlying 'No, no, do not stay, Run, run, run away' confirming that she needs to leave, but is in two minds: 'The more I think the worse I guess, The more I guess the worse I am'.

'Have Mercy' (Mann) (4:55)
This delicate and steady ballad is set up beautifully on the intro and given the full rein of 1980s power in the chorus. It's a lament from someone whose partner makes them feel second best. She knows she can do better, 'The love that I gave him is gone', but he has a habit of winning her over. She feels responsible for making him the way he is. She loved him too much, but 'never thought my love was wasted'. There's acknowledgement that she has a choice, 'You spend your love, Or you conserve it', but she's had enough of his abuse: 'Its hard to hear him curse my name'. She's strong enough to extricate herself, staying positive in the knowledge that she doesn't deserve this treatment. Overall, it's an empowering anthem for making changes that are needed once things turn bad.

The verses are sparse with keys and guitar, well-judged lines adding to the whole, while the chorus is wonderfully harmonised. Holmes gets a more forthright solo after the second chorus and the pacing is well thought-through.

'Sleeping and Waking' (Hausman, Holmes, Mann, Pesce) (3:24)
Another full-band co-write, the bouncy energy driven by Holmes' reverb-laden guitar. It again acknowledges the damage done by a thoughtless ex – 'So fun time is over, but just for the record, It was a little too rough', the understatement with the lightness of the music giving an even darker edge. Her dreams are in pieces and she has had enough, unable to fathom what he is getting from the relationship:

Tell me what love is
Or rather what you expected
Because I've often wondered
What you did not get

The following verse is interesting, ending every line with 'I' as a precursor to the next. After they split, she's at home alone, 'Saying things that were never said, Through the longest night, The longest day', – the classic situation of trying to piece together emotional conversations and coming up with perfect responses that remained unsaid.

'Angels Never Call' (Mann) (3:40)

Quite a delicate number, bass supporting the vocal melody. The chorus gets the full treatment, although it is weaker than others on the album and as a whole feels slightly superficial. The chorus is repeated too frequently, although with variations, and the arrangement lacks the dynamism found elsewhere. There's a feel of filler, not unpleasant, but in this company, it's a little lacking.

Sung from the male perspective, it chronicles his love ('I used to watch her sleep, An angel on vacation'), but she was unable to reciprocate and kept her heart 'locked up tight'. There's a brilliantly funny/sad couplet in 'I guess I beat myself to death, Against her lovely face'.

'No One Is Watching You Now' (Mann) (3:52)

With a plaintive alternating guitar chord opening, it's a great performance from Aimee, reaching for the heights in the chorus before the arrangement builds into the second verse. The backing is sparse enough to make it all about the vocal. She pulls it off with style, and almost surprising power in the bridge before falling back to the stripped-down verse.

A relationship has ended, most likely Aimee and Hausman's. The streets are the same, 'Every corner defined by the places you'd be, But no one is watching you now, Like I did'. There's regret in 'Even the longest days, You could make disappear', and an acknowledgement of his desirability to others – 'The eyes of the girls followed you all around'. Her sadness for herself is now an ache to have him back.

It's a great way to finish, punchy with a beautiful dynamic, capped off by Aimee's best vocal performance on the album.

Related Tracks:

'Sign Of Love' (Jennifer Condos, Mark Goldenberg) (3:50)

Featured (briefly) in the 1987 comedy movie *Back to the Beach*, this is a pop classic that should have been – although not written by Aimee and seemingly recorded as a favour to a friend. The delicate, baroque keyboard intro sparks into a tasty guitar riff on a driving rhythm. Aimee sounds comfortable and the chorus is irresistible. The bridge is strong too and it stands out a mile from a lot of the other stuff of the day. It's a shame it didn't take off; it could have been the band's saviour (even though Aimee was now moving in a different direction).

'When He Puts His Head Down' (Mann) (3:19)

Nice, upbeat and fun. Played as an encore on the *Welcome Home* tour, it shows the band continuing to develop, with a great contribution from Robert Holmes.

'Yesterday' (Mann) (3:26)

Played live in 1987, it appeared as a B-side in Japan. Sarah Brightman recorded it as 'Yesterday (You Stopped Crying)' for her 1990 album *As I Came of Age*. It's a good song with a typically strong chorus, described on stage by Aimee as 'About waking up one morning and finding that your old friend misery has finally left you – it's something that rarely happens to me!'. It, therefore, appears to be a song of optimism for a change!

Everything's Different Now (1988)

Personnel:
Aimee Mann: Vocals, Bass Guitar, Acoustic Guitar
Michael Hausman: Drums and Percussion, Programming
Robert Holmes: Guitars, Background Vocals
Michael Montes: Keyboards
Haeryung Shin: Violin
Peter Abrams: French Horn
Marcus Miller: Additional Bass
Elvis Costello: Background Vocals
Tiger Okoshi: Trumpet & Horn Arrangement
Hal Crook: Trombone
Mike Denneen: Additional Keyboards
Producers: Rhett Davies, Bruce Lampcov
Record Label: Epic Records
Recorded: Blue Jay Recording; Bearsville Studios; Power Station; Q Division
Released: 15 June 1988
Running Time: 39:43
Highest chart place: US:124, UK: -

Joey Pesce left 'Til Tuesday after *Welcome Home* to follow his own creative path. He played in several different bands (including Still Life) and performed solo acoustic guitar shows before teaching himself sculpting (when his son was an infant and too easily awakened by music). He has become an accomplished artist and art conservator, working in many media. Examples of his work are available at pescesculpture.com. Michael Montes was brought in to replace Joey, the band now touring with Dave Darby on bass for much of the set, freeing Aimee to concentrate on singing.

When 'Til Tuesday went back into the studio, the result was a deeply personal and specific collection of songs, mainly written by Mann who was now in control of the songwriting. Michael Hausman co-wrote two tracks with her, but there are no contributions from the other band members. For the first time, outside writers were involved, but completely on Mann's terms. This included Jules Shear, who she'd been in a relationship with since around the release of *Voices Carry*, the ending of this liaison deeply influencing the material on *Everything's Different Now*. Mann insisted to the *Boston Globe* that not every song was about their relationship, 'But I guess they refer to emotions that can be traced back to him'. It's clear that Aimee did not want it to end, as the *LA Times* noted: 'What comes through in these gentle but not too genteel pop songs is a profound sense of, above all, disappointment', seeing her viewpoint as 'unusually self-analytical and mature for one so presumably racked with pain, making for a lovely, insightful, occasionally heartbreaking piece of work'. 'It was a rough situation', Mann told *The Globe*. 'When it was roughest, I didn't write at all, and that contributed to this record taking so long.'

Shear co-wrote one song with Mann and one with Matthew Sweet. Aimee co-wrote two with British ex-pat Kit Hain, while one was written with Declan MacManus, more famous as Elvis Costello. By this point he'd released a dozen albums, achieving success on both sides of the Atlantic, and Aimee had been a fan for many years.

Dealing largely with ending relationships, the album could have become something of a bleak-fest. But as always, the quality of the writing, a surfeit of hooks, and Aimee's ability to make sad songs sound upbeat, made for a great album. It's the least 1980s sounding entry in the 'Til Tuesday catalogue, a confident work built around a songwriter who had found her voice and was working to her own vision. *Everything's Different Now* showed the development in her songwriting and she was much happier with it, primarily because, compared to the debut, she felt it made a more personal statement about her life.

Taking more influence from folk than new wave pop, it has a more acoustic edge. Epic's view was, ''This acoustic guitar music. It will never happen''. 'Of course the next year Tracy Chapman sold like four thousand million records and the Indigo Girls record came out – acoustic guitars everywhere.'

It's easily my favourite of the three 'Til Tuesday releases. But despite critical praise, it again failed commercially, reaching only a lowly 124 in the US album charts, largely due to Epic failing to promote it. Aimee noted that it was 'completely, astonishingly unsupported'. Not enamoured with the new direction, Epic tried again to get Aimee to work with a 'hit doctor'. She refused as that would've furthered the 'music-as-product' view that she hated, a stance that would always bring conflict with major labels. Epic's lack of interest saw the singles fail to make any impression and the album quickly slid out of view. In 1993, Aimee made the following comment to *Musician*:

We went to radio stations and very few people were playing the record. The people that did said nobody had sent it to them; they'd read somewhere we'd put something out and then went out and found it. I felt neglected. I didn't want to put my heart and soul into making a great record and then have nobody hear it. I could have done a better job out of my own home with some stamps. I'm the artist; my job is the art part of it, your job is the selling part.

This marked the start of Aimee's three-year battle to escape from her contract with Epic, which so fuelled her early solo writing. A 1993 interview with *Q Magazine* showed her bitterness:

It's not difficult to figure out that the way to promote me is to put my songs on alternative radio, but to some of these guys, it was like trying to figure out the cure for cancer. They didn't think they could sell whatever it was I was doing, so they wanted me to change fairly drastically to give them a more marketable product. I objected and said 'Maybe you should just let me off the label', but they didn't want to do that either, because they thought that I was just accessible enough – that if I was at a company that really cared about what I was doing, I might be successful. And they didn't want to see that happen. So I was just kept in limbo for three and a half years. And finally, they released me after they were pretty sure my career was ended.

AllMusic praised the band's evolution away from 'Infectious, synth-soaked pop/rock' and desire to challenge themselves and grow with each release, noting that this final album, although lacking the immediacy of *Voices Carry*, was more intimate than *Welcome Home*, while just as rewarding.

As Aimee took more control, it was the last straw for Robert Holmes. He and Michael Montes left after recording *Everything's Different Now*, but before its release, hence the cover art featuring only Mann and Hausman. Although the band had effectively broken up, they supported the album touring as a quintet, featuring Jon Brion and Clayton Scoble but not as permanent members. Multi-instrumentalist, Brion, was by now Aimee's boyfriend and he would play a major role in the early part of her solo career. These later shows featured unusual cover songs and re-worked versions of 'Til Tuesday material, including a grungy dismantling of 'Voices Carry' with the lyrical change 'He said, "Shut up!", I said, "Fuck off!".

After 'Til Tuesday, Robert Holmes 'wanted to rock out' and formed Ultra Blue, where he was finally able to show the full extent of his prodigious guitar skills. The band won Best New Artist at the Boston Music Awards in 1989 but never made it big. He then formed Love Bomb in Vermont before returning to the UK, where he now lives in the Cotswolds, working as a freelance guitarist and playing with blues band The Achievers.

Michael Montes forged a successful career composing film soundtracks, while Michael Hausman went into artist representation and continues to manage Aimee to this day.

'Everything's Different Now' (Jules Shear, Matthew Sweet) (3:56)

From the strummed acoustic intro, there's already a folky feel. It quickly opens into a full band arrangement with a lovely melody and important keyboard contributions supporting the vocal, enticing the listener in before a chorus that hits the spot. The electric guitar is twangy with a touch of echo, the bridge swooping down beautifully to Aimee's lower vocal register – particularly pleasing in her delivery of the 'A past we hated' line. It's an energetic, upbeat opener.

Written by Jules Shear with Matthew Sweet, it dates from before Jules' and Aimee's breakup, but appears to foreshadow it. Remembering the early days of the relationship – 'You know when love is real, It changes the life that you're living, And now I've found it here, It overcomes my fear, Of holding back instead of giving' – it considers the thrill of finding someone who makes you feel complete. 'When I hear the phone ring your voice pulls me in 'til I'm far

33

away'. The chorus underlines the all-encompassing rush of initial affection, but there's already an awareness that this state of bliss won't last:

Well, soon I'll say your name
And then I'll go insane
I won't understand what I'm thinking
I'll look down at my shoes
I'll wonder what I'll lose
If I feel this consciousness sinking
And we both know what that means
Returning to what we knew before
Forgetting that everything's different now

'Rip In Heaven' (Mann, Kit Hain) (3:31)

Holmes adds a flourish before the verse, taking things to a low-key place of rim shots and keyboard washes. The chorus is supreme, lifting with impact after the beautifully subdued quality of the verse. With a brief Holmes solo before the final chorus with its nice variations, the song ends strongly. It's punchy and a pretty obvious single choice, but it failed to chart – a shame as it deserved a decent hearing and would have appealed to a wider range of listeners than may have been familiar with the band previously.

The lyric opens with an item given to the couple by one set of parents – a 'relic of our history'. There's a homely quality, the words spoken intimately between lovers at the end of the road who still hold an affection for each other. 'To tell the truth, It wasn't bad, We had to have a reason, And lack of love wasn't it'. They both know that their present is lacking 'A future where both of us can fit'. The regret is voiced in the 'Sorry, Darling' chorus where 'I was counting to forever, And never even got to ten' – the initial view of 'heaven' always out of reach. The second verse is worded with tenderness and a wonderful analogy for how feelings can alter through over-analysis:

It's funny how you just assume
You're going to work it out
Or give it at least a try
But optimistic feelings can't be
Passed from hand to hand
You handle them they tend to die

Co-writer Kit Hain had found success with the duo Marshall Hain in the late-1970s, reaching the Top Three in the UK with 'Dancing in the City' before moving to the US to become an in-demand songwriter.

'Why Must I' (Mann) (3:42)

With hints of Bruce Hornsby, the driving intro, superbly realised by guitar, bass and drums, moves on a keyboard melody into strident chords and the first verse. Aimee's voice is strong with a lilting quality to the higher parts as the melody rises and falls. Holmes stalks around, adding detail in country style, a relaxed solo winding around Aimee's vocal in the extended second chorus. It's a polished arrangement from a band that knows what they're doing. Montes' choices are excellent, particularly the hook line, and it fades quite beautifully with Holmes again showing what an asset he is.

This is one of my favourite songs here, opening up a view of where Aimee's career would head. In 'Rip In Heaven' it sounds like the protagonist is the one who is most aware that the relationship has run its course. This is the flipside with despair around lines like 'Why must I take it so hard?' and 'There's no light in the tunnel or dog in the yard'. There's self-blame in 'It's my fault for wanting too much', with the awareness that life will just carry on blighted by the sadness she feels. Other people deal with these situations 'With either bourbon or God', but she has made him her whole world. It's the way she is, but she implores herself to 'Be careful of the love you find'. Ultimately there's anger in 'Do you think I enjoy it?' when confronted with the suggestion that she's a willing victim of her own failings.

'J For Jules' (Mann) (4:26)
A change of pace, as yearning multi-layered French horn, from Peter Abrams, takes us into the verse. Quiet and sedate, a basic arrangement of bass and drum machine accents the vocals. Keyboard strings fill it out, guitar coming in for the sweeping chorus, lifting elegantly before the low-key verse, claustrophobic and filled with pain. The chorus releases the tension, like the singer being freed from the failing relationship. The bridge is a lovely change, horn returning to end brightly with Aimee floating in the high register.

There's no hiding the meaning here, and Jules Shear figures largely. One of the first songs written after their breakup, Aimee remembered staying with a friend. 'He had an old Martin guitar and I played four chords on it and immediately broke down crying', she told *The Boston Globe*. Those are the chords on 'J For Jules'. When I later sat down to write it, it just came out. It was like writing a letter to somebody. It was already in the air.'

From the intimate details of the first verses, a couple happy in each other's company, prepare for sleep in 'a country that began with a 'J' for Jules'. This likening of the relationship to a country seems telling; is it a sign of a one-sided affair? It is not clear from whose perspective the chorus comes. 'You know I'll miss you ... But I'll release you ... Someday we'll be happy again'. The next verse is a strange one; the 'rain' never comes, you have so few blessings that you can count them on your thumbs, and sleeping dogs just want to be left alone. It suggests that things aren't right, but nothing is being done to resolve the situation.

Received wisdom seems to show that 'There's no way a country like that' – so all-encompassing – 'could die', but it's a lie, and the metaphorical car that she bought isn't going anywhere. 'The country that began with a 'J', Now ends in my heart' – a poignant couplet as the song culminates with a repeated 'Someday we'll be happy again'.

The *LA Times* noted Mann 'wearing her heart on her sleeve – and she wears it well'. Of the direct nature of the title, she told *The Globe*, 'Yes, it made him a little uncomfortable to have his name on a song, but he's not in a position to complain'.

'(Believed You Were) Lucky' (Mann, Jules Shear) (3:38)

Another Jules Shear co-write, this single only reached number 95. The scratchy acoustic opening suggests simplicity, the vocal arriving with basic keyboard support. It's subdued, but the vocal line carries it beautifully, picking up the pace and building the arrangement as it heads to the fantastic chorus – full, punchy and a real earworm – the verses counteracting it to fine effect.

There's a sense of hopelessness in the first verses. It's an uphill struggle with no point in carrying on alone, seeming to stem from Jules' indecision: 'It was a really amazing relationship', she told *The Boston Globe*, 'I thought it was very healthy to stay together, but Jules just couldn't make up his mind'. It requires consensus to carry the flame, otherwise 'It won't burn the same'. It seems obvious, but it comes with a realisation that the other party might never have felt the same way, leading to the chorus:

I wish you believed in life
Believed in fate
Believed you were lucky
And worth the wait
'Cause life could be lovely
Life could be so great

Ultimately, what's done is done and it's time to move on. 'I'll change my mind again, You change your address'. The bridge offers some hope for the future, but with a sting remaining in the present:

There must be some other door that they are saving
Behind which my happiness lies
I won't be wasting my words
To tell you hopes that I had

The surprise dropping of the F-bomb in the alternate last line of the final chorus underlines the passion of the delivery and the magnitude of what they appear to have let slip away. It was obviously dropped from the accompanying video which featured a frizzy and spiky-haired Aimee (not her best look) strumming guitar while a cello in a picture frame is bowed by a saw. Many of the visuals from the album cover appear, often literally interpreting the lyrics. It all looks a bit disjointed. Hausman and Jon Brion turn up in support and there's lots of green screen that now looks dated, but the song still holds up.

'Limits To Love' (Mann) (3:36)

Another unusual song, with brushed drums, rim shots and leading bass building a sparse arrangement for Aimee to relay the tale of someone who just cannot take advice.

There's plenty of story in the lyric structure. Does it talk about an acquaintance? Or is it turned back on Aimee, seen from the perspective of friends, or herself? The opening 'I've known her ever since she was a kid' suggests the latter, delivered with an awareness that she keeps repeating mistakes. Have her friends given up on her because of this, or has she given up on herself? There's only so much advice you can offer when someone is hell-bent on ignoring it. She's loved, but there's only so far that can go: 'I guess her definition of a friend, Was someone long on love and short on advice'. In the end, 'She'll get in trouble, but she will scrape through, She's the kind of girl who can always find help', with an awareness that her poor judgement doesn't come from stupidity: 'You've got to be smart if you're fooling yourself'.

Keys and guitars arrive as the song slides easily into the one-line chorus. The simplicity is deceptive as there's plenty of detail to make it work, carried on the plodding bassline. French horn returns for a quirky and winning contribution, strings joining towards the end with a gorgeous floating violin part from Haeryung Shin. It's a strange song that settles in nicely and bears many repeated listens.

'Long Gone (Buddy)' (Mann, Hausman) (4:34)

Co-written with Michael Hausman, the bass part is striking from the off, Marcus Miller supplying his exemplary chops to give a pleasing funk. Holmes' trademark sheets-of-sound guitars in many ways suggest something more akin to the earlier 'Til Tuesday albums – steady rhythm delivering momentum as Aimee sings strongly, particularly in the high-end on the hooky chorus. The arrangement opens out towards the end, Montes and Holmes free to roam.

The first verse has a forthright matter-of-factness about it; we've made a mess of the situation and it's painful to deal with, but there's never any comfort to be had from the truth. 'Nobody wants to be happier more than I do, But happiness, I must confess, I don't have'. The chorus of 'It's long gone, buddy, now – run and go after it' suggests that all the love that the relationship once had is finished ('That love is gone, That love is blind, That love is so unkind'), and he needs to make himself gone too. She's not afraid of being alone, despite the pain – everything happens for a reason, although she 'Can't understand for the moment what this could mean'.

'The Other End (Of The Telescope)' (Mann, Declan MacManus) (3:53)

Of this collaboration with Declan MacManus, Aimee said, 'I'm embraced by those interested in songwriters and not by those interested in attitude. For them, evidence of craftsmanship betrays attitude'. In 1994 she described to Ian Ravendale how she 'got up the nerve to send him the song and asked 'Would you, possibly, if you have the time', and he sent it back!'. Declan recorded his own version for his 1996 album *All This Useless Beauty*.

The wordiest track on the album, it's elegant and folk-edged, showing the direction that Aimee was moving towards. It's warm and well-arranged, not swamping the melody, the chorus lush with Declan's backing vocals, suitably set back to give depth. Aimee's performance is superb, powerful and confident. French horn appears again, and Montes' contribution is excellent, knowing where to place himself to best effect.

Another relationship bites the dust, discussion of the whys or wherefores irrelevant – it's time to decide on future paths. The words turning to smoke, lost in the air ('There's always something smouldering somewhere') and there are some beautiful lines here:

> The sky was just phosphorus stars hung on strings
> And you swore that they'd always be mine
> When you can pull them down anytime

The words of enduring love covered up the fragile and precarious nature of the relationship. 'The answer was under your nose, But the question never arose'. The pair need to be apart, but there's hope that they won't be complete strangers and 'You'll see me off in the distance, I hope, At the other end of the telescope'. A live version later appeared as a B-side several times, and as part of a special edition of Aimee's solo debut, *Whatever*.

'Crash And Burn' (Mann, Kit Hain) (4:46)

From the plaintive first verse, the chorus sweeps in to lift the tempo, Holmes adding some fine contributions, including a well-judged solo after the second chorus. Less hooky than other songs here, it's another mature work.

There are some heavy lyrical jabs and a deep sense of anger and resentment, as in the first verse:

> He was saying, 'You look like an angel'
> But you never really know what the hell to make of that
> Take your pick 'cause it don't really matter
> I get lonely when I hear it and sad when he takes it back
> But all in all, another fall won't even make a dent

There's an inevitability to the crash, with an acceptance that 'That kind of thing is easier to say than do'. Another damning couplet comes in 'You keep saying that you're only human, What you mean is that you think you're the only human here'. The pain is clear to see, with a plea to break with tradition and 'We'll pretend we're everything that you believe we're not'. Sad.

'How Can You Give Up?' (Mann, Hausman) (3:38)

Another Hausman co-write, and another appearance from Marcus Miller, also featuring jazz musicians Tiger Okoshi (trumpet and arrangement), and Berklee professor, Hal Crook (trombone). Additional keys come from Mike Denneen, who worked on several of Aimee's solo albums.

A song of waning confidence in the face of a love affair becoming more difficult to sustain, but with a question as to how the other party can give up on it so easily; 'You ought to know love is hard to find'. The next verse comes across like the other party giving themselves a pep talk; 'Steady, Hold your breath, It isn't over yet, So with one small admission you're paying the price'. But there's another sting in 'Did you tell yourself lying was good advice?'.

The rhythms feel dated, but the chorus is upbeat with a winning hook, Holmes adding another brief yet fine solo. The brass is somewhat buried in the arrangement until right at the end, which is a shame. The song itself is a bit lightweight, making it a strange way to end such a confident and powerful album.

Related Tracks

'Do It Again' (Mann, Hausman) (3:57)

An outtake from *Everything's Different Now*, it found a home as a bonus on the 1996 *Coming Up Close* retrospective. An upbeat acoustic guitar colours it, drums kicking in with the second verse. It's pretty stripped back, not as reliant on 1980s production values, and with little in the way of keyboards.

The first verse is sung from the male perspective, as a couple discuss a familiar situation where it seems that the chances of the relationship succeeding are slender. At a restaurant, she looks in a mirror and sees herself looking back – the situation hasn't changed. The third verse is back to him:

Time is all we need, she finally let out
But I see her drawing maps if she can get out
Now I wonder which of us will get the axe out
And do the final blow

It's just a matter of time before one of them is going to call an end to it. It's a pleasant song, but nothing overly special.

'Time Stand Still' (Geddy Lee, Alex Lifeson, Neil Peart) (5:09)

Aimee's contribution to this song by Canadian giants, Rush, gave her a higher profile in the UK than she had previously enjoyed. Released in 1987, credited to 'Rush (featuring Aimee Mann)', the single from Rush's *Hold Your Fire* album spent three weeks on the UK chart, peaking at number 42. As a huge Rush fan, this was the first time I had encountered Aimee. She made a huge impact, both on the record and during the supporting live shows where her image appeared on the giant screen behind the band to accompany her taped vocals.

The song is particularly catchy, stylistically typical of Rush's keyboard-heavy mid-1980s material. Aimee sings alongside Geddy Lee, adding the lilting title refrain in the chorus, the only time Rush ever featured another lead vocalist. The accompanying video is a fun studio romp, with Aimee filming the band in action, accompanied by lots of now very dated effects.

Regarding her involvement, Aimee told *Guitar World*, 'I'm not sure if they had heard a song of mine or someone told them about me, but they contacted my manager at the time and asked me if I wanted to sing on it. I didn't know Rush's stuff that much but I thought, "Why not?". I liked the song and thought the part was really pretty. Originally, Geddy Lee was singing it. He's got such a powerful voice and I remember saying to him, "Dude, your falsetto is so great. You shouldn't have me". But they really wanted to have a different singer on it. I'm very proud that I had that opportunity'.

Aimee On Songwriting

Before diving into Aimee's solo career, it's worth discussing her songwriting methodology. In 2015, she said at a live event in LA, 'You can't be too precious and think that your whole reputation rests on it. Just write a song, it can be about your cat, your friend or whatever, no one has to hear it', conveying the sense of doing it for yourself and not worrying about the results – it only needs to be released 'into the wild' when you're happy.

From her early days, Aimee needed to understand the mechanics of songwriting and put the work in to learn her craft, looking to others to discover what they knew and develop herself further. She was drawn to liberated writers with their own voices, like Elvis Costello, Squeeze's Chris Difford and Glenn Tilbrook, and individualists like XTC's Andy Partridge and Ray Davies of The Kinks.

As for content, 'I like to get inside situations, search for answers. Songs are explorations, trying to gain understanding, getting to the bottom of it. Some people look away, but I believe facing it is what makes it better. It's what you don't know that hurts you the most. I'm a person who wants to know'. However, it's not all about facing up to problems: 'Writing songs is the most fun because that's the part that never has to be anyone else's. I don't have to have any motivation aside from "I feel like it". There's something really cool about that'. So why release records? 'Because I'm a songwriter and a singer and this is the only thing I know how to do. For some who listen, it's valuable and that justifies my existence. You never know how, and if, what you're doing is going to be helpful and comforting to someone. I've definitely had people come up to me after shows and say "Your music has helped me through some tough times", and that's valuable.'

She described to *Guitar World* in 2017 how her songwriting process usually began 'by having some kind of melody idea or chord progression. If there's something interesting that stands out, I'll say to myself, "OK, what does this music sound like? What's its emotional centre and what kind of story would suit that centre?". Then I'll figure out where I intersect with that kind of narrative'.

'I try to make the lyrics conversational and report the facts. The other thing that's to my taste is very clever lyrics, but I'm not so good at those.' When asked by *The Performing Songwriter* in 1999 whether she has to work hard to produce them, she said 'It depends on how bad my writer's block is! I find that jotting down ideas in a notebook – which I'll occasionally do when I want to get into the writing process – really helps. It's the kind of thing I should probably utilise more than I actually do. For me, it's usually just a matter of writing down topics, rather than individual phrases. But something like that can really jump-start the creative process, especially when you don't feel like writing at all'.

Aimee's songs are considered dark, miserable and filled with disappointment, stemming from a combination of her personality and experiences: 'At heart,

I really am a very optimistic person. That's why I'm constantly disappointed'. The human condition fascinates her and the complexity of trying to combine individuals into jointly beneficial relationships is fraught with difficulties, giving endless fuel for songs. Failing love affairs is not the entirety of her subject matter, however, and there are interesting tangents on the journey through her discography. In 1993, she told *Time Out*:

> Songs are the perfect form for exploring things. Novels, short stories are probably beyond me. But songwriting form is simple, and by its limitations, it makes the job easy for me. And working within limitations I find much more liberating than to have no limits at all. What's great about song form is that it's somebody talking to you. Directly to you. And you have a moment of recognition. That's art, right there. A moment of recognition.

Perhaps unusually for a female singer-songwriter, she has a significant male following, which she puts down to her approach being 'a little more masculine' than the norm; refusing to be a victim and being happy to confront wrongdoing – even when she's aiming at herself.

> It's not some special kind of female scorned rage or bitchy wildcat. It's a person who's legitimately angry at being treated badly. I felt that growing up, there was always a stigma in being angry. Women are less often allowed to have those feelings of rage and jealousy. We're supposed to be Mrs Happy all the time.

She has admitted to not having much of an ear for melody before working at it. Throughout her career, melody has been at the heart of what makes her often quirky songs tick, and her recorded work has always shown a deep understanding of what makes a great hook. The counteraction of lyrics that often deal with despair, breakups, endings and the doubt and uncertainty that come with them, are set against music that is often upbeat, fun and catchy, and the dichotomy adds a delicious extra layer to the songs.

The art of songwriting still fascinates her, and throughout 2019, she and her latter-day musical collaborator, Ted Leo, hosted a bi-weekly podcast, *The Art of Process*, where, through interviews with friends from across the creative spectrum, they discuss how musical ideas are turned into art across an in-depth yet fun and engaging sixteen episodes.

Whatever (1993)

Personnel:
Aimee Mann: Vocals, Acoustic and Electric Guitar, Bass, Mellotron, Pump Organ,
Percussion
Michael Hausman, Jim Keltner and Milt Sutton: Drums and Percussion
Jon Brion: Bass, Electric Guitar, Piano, Chamberlin, Mellotron, Optigan, Pump
and Hammond Organs, Toy Piano, Marimba, Vibraphone, Drums and Percussion,
Harmonica, Piccolo, Background Vocals
Buddy Judge: Acoustic Guitar, Background Vocals, Pipes
Todd Nelson: Electric Guitar
Randy Brion: Euphonium, Trombone
Mike Breaux: Bassoon, Oboe
Roger McGuinn: 12-string Electric Guitar, Background Vocals
David Coleman: Cello, Electric Cello
Sid Sharp, Joy Lyle, Harry Shirinian, Harry Shultz: Strings
Producers: Tony Berg, Jon Brion, Michael Hausman, Aimee Mann
Record Label: Imago Records (original release); Geffen (reissue)
Recorded: Q Division, Capitol Studios, Clubhouse, Blue Jay, Bearsville, Zeitgeist,
Sunset Sound, Presence
Released: 11 May 1993
Running Time: 52:14
Highest chart place: US:127, UK:39

It seems that a fourth 'Til Tuesday album was recorded in demo form. After it
was rejected by Epic, a number of the songs were used on Aimee's debut solo
album, *Whatever*, some of the material dating back as far as 1989. As well as
refusing to release anything further from the band, Epic would not allow Aimee
to walk away from her contract, which left her in a state of limbo.

She changed her look during this period, shunning the early sex-bomb glitz
in favour of a more comfortable 'anti-fashion' style. As she said to *The Boston
Globe* in 1990: 'The image shift is that nobody cares about image anymore. It's
much more music-for-musicians or music made for ourselves. I wear the same
clothes onstage I wear to the show. I wear my glasses now so I can see what
I'm doing. It's a huge amount of freedom'. Aimee still gigged regularly in the
Boston area, continuing to use the 'Til Tuesday name for some time, eventually
retiring it during the recording of the new album. She told *Musician* at the
time 'We used a couple of different drummers besides Michael, and since he's
the only other original member of 'Til Tuesday, it seemed best to call it a solo
record.'

'It's hard to look for a new label when you're not really off another one but
you're not really on it either', she said, shortly before the release of *Whatever*.
It took four years to sort out the situation, during which she evolved her
sound, taking in more folk and underground influences. Her antipathy to Epic
(and parent company CBS) was clear in 1995, when she told the BBC: 'It's a

major surprise to me that no artist has ever taken the elevator up to the 32nd floor of the CBS Building and sprayed the entire place with machine-gun fire'.

She eventually managed to buy herself out of the contract 'for a huge bunch of cash'. Giant Records – started by industry heavyweight, Irving Azoff – offered a deal. But after months of discussion – on the day that Aimee signed – Giant backed out, leading to other industry players deciding that the problem must be with her. 'Now when anyone is labelled a difficult artist, I think "Ah, a person of integrity." With her then-manager Patrick Rains putting up the money, it was decided to continue with the recording and then look for a label when the album was finished, thus giving her full artistic control and 'a great opportunity to experiment'. Assisted by people she trusted, without a deal in place, 'nobody got near the money they were used to getting. They just did it because they wanted to be involved in it. It was really a labour of love on all parts'.

Whatever was constructed with the help of Jon Brion; first-time producer, latter-day 'Til Tuesday bandmate and now ex-boyfriend. Brion played on it extensively and co-wrote several of the songs. When asked about working with him, she replied 'the things that are in the back of your mind, he can play them'. Regarding writing together, it was akin to utilising 'two halves of the same brain'. As she told the *LA Times*:

I don't want to be perceived as this languishing girl crying a song whenever her boyfriend leaves. I write about relationships, but sometimes a song is ironic or from another perspective. Boy-girl is more narrow than my scope. For example, it could also be between parent and child. It's always helpful to have anything that indicates to you you're not alone in this particular kind of wretchedness.

Mann's voice was now richer than on the 'Til Tuesday recordings, often utilising lower tones. The album sessions and Brion's involvement saw her sound become warmer, partly from the use of analogue keyboards, Optigans, Mellotrons and Chamberlins giving *Whatever* an intriguing and distinctive feel that belies its somewhat throwaway title. As she said, 'The great thing about those instruments, and one of the main concepts for this record, is contrast. Not only between high and low fidelity but between current sounds and instant history, like a crackly recording of some ancient violin player.'

The album sleeve features Mann, all in black, sprawled on the floor. On the reverse, she's sitting up and looking at the camera, the inlay featuring a close-up of her smiling and a photo of her among sand-dunes. Art direction was by Gail Marowitz, a collaboration that still persists.

With the album nearly completed, Aimee signed with Imago Records. Upon release in May 1993, reviews were predominantly favourable. *Rolling Stone* labelled her 'The patron saint of smart women making foolish choices', praising the 'sunny, surreal melodies' and evocative lyrical content. *The Chicago Tribune* offered comparisons to Elvis Costello, and *Spin* described the juxtaposition of the upbeat guitar pop sound with the bleakness of the words as 'melodically a sorceress, lyrically an emotional train wreck'. As *Musician* noted, 'What's surprising is that such unpleasant subjects as despair, defeat and revenge, should translate into exciting, listener-friendly music – a melodious testament to the craft of pop songwriting and an intelligent reflection on the many problems musicians can encounter'. The album peaked at 39 on the UK charts, but despite positive reviews, it sold only modestly in the US, reaching 127 in *Billboard*.

The album's failure was partly due to issues being faced by Imago Records. They had built a roster of influential alternative artists, but fell into serious financial difficulties, exacerbated in December 1994 when Bertelsmann Music Group (BMG – one of the 'big five' record companies of the time) withdrew its backing. With the loss of its distribution, Imago filed for bankruptcy.

On the perceived issue of band members going solo, Aimee told *The Journal News* in 1993, 'For people who didn't hear the last two records, it doesn't make any sense and they find it a little annoying even, I understand that. If the lead singer of Berlin came out with a solo album, I'd say, "Yeah, right, I'm sure it's going to be a masterpiece." Same thing, it's the same era, same kind of haircut'.

A double CD version of *Whatever* emerged in 1994, subtitled *An Exclusive Collection*, featuring previously released B-sides and live tracks. In the longer term, *Whatever* has been held up as something of a classic, included in the book *1001 Albums You Must Hear Before You Die* in 2010.

Mann opened for World Party in the UK and played solo gigs before supporting The Kinks in the US. On 15 November 1993, she played *The Bottom Line* in New York City with a band that included former XTC guitarist, Dave Gregory (who she dated for a while). XTC member, Andy Partridge, was in the audience and joined them on stage for the encore, singing and playing tambourine for a cover of his band The Dukes of Stratosphear's 'Collideascope'. This was a significant event, as he had been absent from live performance since his breakdown in 1982. Of the occasion, Mann said in *Rolling Stone*, 'I figured once he heard me sing it and not do a very good job, he'd push me out of the way and start singing, which is pretty much what happened'.

In April 2020, a live collection of radio broadcasts from 1993 and 1994 appeared under the title *Clean Slate*. It featured eleven tracks, seven *Whatever* songs (with some duplication) and a cover of Dave Edmunds' 'Girls Talk'.

During the recording of *Whatever*, Aimee met singer-songwriter Michael Penn (brother of actors Sean and Chris). She moved to the West Coast to be with him in 1995 and they married in 1997.

'I Should've Known' (Mann) (4:53)

The album's single (in a shortened 4:11 'Radio Edit') did reasonably well, reaching 16 on the *Billboard* Modern Rock chart. The UK release in August 1993 got to number 55, doing slightly better at 45 when reissued in March

1994. It was Aimee's first UK chart entry since 'Time Stand Still' in 1987. A live version appeared on a UK 10" EP.

The percussion, woozy guitar and keyboard intro coalesce into strident chords. It's a grabber, the chorus harmony vocals the icing on the cake. As an opener, it hits the spot harder than most of Aimee's songs to date, and with a directness that forcefully lays down her solo credentials. The bridge is followed by soaring guitar, which continues with yelping vocals to the smooth ending figure, fading to nothing on extraneous sounds.

It's a forthright lyric too, full of clear-as-day realisations that a relationship was bound to end badly – and given her difficulties with Epic, it's probably about that. Things look better now that the dust has settled, she feels invigorated and confident after shedding the pain. There's bitterness, but with a sense of relief: 'I should thank you almost, No one could kill it off until you bled it'. The line highlights a persistent betrayal that eventually became too much, taking over the façade that the relationship was working as everyday life got in the way of the truth: 'I should have known you would betray me but without the kiss'. It's a song built on harsh experience but underlines the feeling of being stronger as a result.

Unable to make the song work, it eventually came together with the help of Bob Clearmountain at the mixing stage. The video, filmed near Ithaca, NY, sees Aimee running around the house, filling a basket with the detritus of a failed relationship, then heading outside on a wintry evening to burn it on a bonfire, excitedly opening a bottle of champagne. Back in the house, she sings whilst reading, drinking tea and having dinner. A cake decorated with Grant Woods' *American Gothic* painting is cut and consumed. Aimee then plays a fictional *Monopoly*-like board game called *Monobstacle,* with some ventriloquist's dummies, before shooting them with a tiny pistol. And if you ever want to see Aimee riding a bicycle, this is a good place to start. Director Katherine Dieckmann noted that 'Aimee wanted to break out of the whole 'Til Tuesday image of the heartbroken, lovesick girl raging about relationships, so we decided to treat this breakup with some black humour. I was pushing more of the angry woman thing with the whole burning of the boyfriend's stuff. But Aimee wanted it to be funny, like "Thank you; you did me the biggest favour by leaving"'.

'Fifty Years After The Fair' (Mann) (3:46)

A remembrance of the 1939 World's Fair in New York, as if from a grandparent's perspective. Images of the event are featured, including the Trylon and Perisphere (modernistic structures that were central to the Flushing Meadow site), as the song considers the bright new future that the fair foresaw. After the hard times of the 1930s, hope was needed, but 50 years later, the reality of that future had not measured up: 'I guess just for a second we thought that all good things would rise to the top.' The chorus refrain of 'How beautiful it was tomorrow, We'll never have a day of sorrow' highlights that flicker of hope. Though it was soon snuffed out, despite the 'decades ahead of us to get it right' – the reality of how little of this bright new world actually came to pass, looming large. Ironically, within six months of the fair's grand opening – and while the event was still open – World War II started.

There's a jaunty and upbeat feel, full of wide-eyed optimism, carried on the guitar line. The harmony vocals and the instrumental extension at the end are a delight. Jim Keltner plays drums, and the Byrds', Roger McGuinn, appears with trademark 12-string to add to the late-1960s vibe, alongside Mellotron and Chamberlin. Aimee recalled Jon Brion attempting to imitate McGuinn to the point that 'Maybe we should just call the real thing. But the real thing didn't sound anything like the imitation'. A 1989 demo was included in the *Exclusive Collection* and used as a European B-side.

'4th Of July' (Mann) (3:21)
In 2000, Elvis Costello included *Whatever* (with specific reference to this song) in a feature of '500 albums that can improve your life' for *Vanity Fair*. He said in interviews that he wished he'd written the opening lines, 'Today's the 4th of July, Another June has gone by, And when they light up our town I just think what a waste of gunpowder and sky'.

The song is sung with simple acoustic guitar accompaniment. Delicate Mellotron enters in soothing support, Hausman's drums added for the chorus. It's ethereal with a quiet melancholy, a sense of homesickness perhaps, after a breakup where she ponders on whether her ex-lover will eventually realise that he should have treated her better:

My God, I should have told her
What would it take?
But, now here I am and the world's gotten colder
And she's got the river down which I sold her

However, she's aware that the path she's following is just 'Another chapter in a book where the chapters are endless', and, heartbreakingly, 'They're always the same.' String embellishments appear, but at the core, it's a heartfelt voice and guitar folk song. A live version was included in the *Exclusive Collection*.

'Could've Been Anyone' (Music: Mann, Jules Shear, Marty Willson-Piper, Lyrics: Mann) (4:23)
Co-written with old flame, Jules Shear, and Marty Willson-Piper (from The Church and All About Eve), probably in 1989 after the duo teamed up to record Shear's *The Third Party* album.

The words consider that the fault of this particular failed relationship sits squarely with the other party, and it would've happened to anyone in the same position, ending with a resolute 'I think that's enough now', drawing the matter to a close.

From the off, guitars jangle pleasingly, with slashing chords adding grit. The chorus is forceful, with harmonies and antique keyboard additions, McGuinn appearing again with inimitable Byrdsian 12-string. The bridge pares things back before launching into a guitar workout, ending in a beautiful crescendo with harmony vocals, Aimee letting rip during the fade. Lovely stuff.

'Put Me On Top' (Mann) (3:28)

Written before the breakup of 'Til Tuesday, 'Most people think it's sexual, but that doesn't bother me. I think it's sort of funny', Aimee told *The Boston Globe* in 1990, confirming that the song is about The Springfields and Velvet Crush drummer, Ric Menck – a 'champion complainer' who thinks the world owes him a living. 'He's a great musician but he whines a lot':

> I should be riding on a float in the hit parade
> Instead of standing on the curb behind the barricade
> Another verse in the doormat serenade

'I tend to get depressed rather than complain about things, but after the song was written, I thought, "You know, this could be my story too".'

The jangly guitar and Mellotron intro leads to a brooding and beautifully delivered first verse. The chorus is bright and full, the album's elements of harmony, keyboard textures and guitars coming together. The bridge of 'Put some hope in the bottom of the box for me, I need it' is the springboard for a brief guitar solo, setting up the final chorus and a long atmospheric fade.

Menck's response was The Springfields' 1991 song, 'Wonder', which ironically came out before Aimee's song was released!

'Stupid Thing' (Mann, Jon Brion) (4:27)

This second single reached number 47 in the UK in November 1993. It seems that early in a relationship, one party decides to break up based on trumped-up accusations, making it sound like the decision was made for them by the other person, thus 'Stopping it all before it even started'.

> Nothing was saving our day
> There was nothing to say
> But you said something anyway
> Claiming I stepped out of line
> Which forced you to leave me
> As if that idea was mine

The organ textures of the intro morph into piano and acoustic guitar, and there's a sad tone to the vocal. As the chorus hits, shards of electric guitar shine through as the arrangement gradually builds, Jim Keltner again on drums. The final verse is particularly biting:

Maybe that's just how I am
To fall where I stand
Or I'm weak for that kind of man
One who looks helpless and brave
But you turned into a coward
I don't care for the parts you saved

Jon Brion's guitar solo has an epic quality, building to a beautiful peak before falling away. The closing section is just fantastic, vocal and guitar entwined with swelling keyboard support.

A live version appeared on the *Exclusive Collection* with an alternate take as a B-side of 'That's Just What You Are'.

'Say Anything' (Mann, Jon Brion) (4:57)
Released as a promo-only single, featuring a 4:02 edit plus an acoustic take. With drums from Milt Sutton, and Mann adding percussion, the bulk of the instrumentation is performed by Jon Brion, including guitars, piano and Mellotron.

There's an air of petulance, the courtroom analogy putting a partner on trial to explain their actions and the obvious lies: 'If you were everything you say, Things would be different today'. Ultimately – 'Say anything, I've heard everything' – things won't change. It has been a long and frustrating road, 'So why do I refuse the truth, When I clearly cannot use the comfort of one more lame excuse'.

The music slowly whirs into action, almost tuning up before a powerful electric guitar chord launches the song. The guitar remains the focus, slashing across the other instruments, with keyboard embellishments adding detail. The chorus harmonies hook the listener into the energy, a cynically engaging vitality. The Beatle-esque horn flourish is a lovely addition before a blazing guitar solo lifts the lid, all ending elegantly amid twinkling keys.

A live version appeared as a 'Stupid Thing' B-side, as did an acoustic version which also featured in the *Exclusive Collection*.

'Jacob Marley's Chain' (Mann) (3:01)
In Charles Dickens' *A Christmas Carol*, the ghost of Jacob Marley is bound in a chain, its links forged from every bad deed he undertook during his life, forcing him to carry the weight of these actions through eternity.

In the song, a friend also feels weighed down under a chain of his own making. But the song is not saying that life is built on sorrow, simply that 'It's just full of thoughts that act as souvenirs', each a reminder to ensure that the pain does not disappear in a metaphorical binding which is simply part of the human condition. The song ends with a shrug that, as the chain exists, 'I think I'd rather just go on to Hell, Where there's a snowball's chance that the personnel, Might help to carry Jacob Marley's chain'.

Buddy Judge's quietly picked guitar introduces the fragile vocal, Aimee at her most intimate. Organ widens the scope as the vocal becomes more forceful. The instrumental section before the fourth verse brings a militaristic rhythm from Hausman's orchestral percussion, suggesting the inexorable march towards oblivion, as the song slows to a beautiful close. The merging tones of Mellotron, pump organ, harmonium and Chamberlin, make this a fine example of the sound variations available on *Whatever*, standing out as a simple, yet highly effective, addition.

'Mr. Harris' (Mann) (4:05)

A song about overcoming societal boundaries placed on dating outside your age group. Wide differences in age generally result in raised eyebrows, and that is the situation here, the singer trying to explain why she is seeing a man old enough to be her father – or grandfather, as there's a suggestion of a 40-year age gap. Her mother voices concern that the singer's looking for a father figure, but she loves him for who he is and looks beyond the obstacles others are putting in the way of their happiness. He dresses in a quaintly old-fashioned way, but he looks after himself. 'His hair is white, but he looks half his age, He looks like Jimmy Stewart in his younger days'. Ultimately they are aware of the reality that 'We've only got ten years or twenty left', but if they're happy, what else really matters? 'Sometimes it takes a lifetime to get what you need'.

There's a homely feel to the instrumentation, led by Brion's piano, with oboe from Mike Breaux winding around the vocal melody. As the song develops with what *Musician* called a 'delicately ironic string arrangement' (again reminiscent of The Beatles), euphonium from Jon's brother Randy makes an appearance, turning it into a fully arranged piece that remains warm and wistful throughout. Aimee's vocal hits the spot, another high point in an album of real depth.

At a concert in 2008, she sang it as a request for the first time in a decade, commenting wryly that 'When I wrote that song, I thought a big age gap did not matter. I don't fucking believe that now!'.

'I Could Hurt You Now' (Mann) (4:17)

There's venom here: 'This is for the one who was false, Who taught me about building walls'. It's payback time for a breach of trust and the hurt caused:

This is for the time that I lost
The death of who I thought I was
The things in which I cannot believe
For fear I'll wear them on my sleeve
Things I know that will never be returned
But I crossed that bridge before it burned

She's still raw, and the anger bubbles through, making it clear that he means nothing to her now and she could do him serious harm for the pain he's brought.

Echoed guitars build tension, released as the chorus hits, the lightness of the melody line set against the brooding instrumentation. Strings again feature, in the shape of David Coleman's electric cello. There's drive throughout, and the instrumental section before the final chorus sees strings, keys and guitar move through repeated lines to the fade.

'I Know There's A Word' (Mann, Jon Brion) (3:16)

A deceptively simple song about trying to come to terms with a situation that can't be unique. There has to be a word to describe it; she just can't recall what it is. But it isn't a good feeling, so when she figures out what the word is, 'I'll write it down in case it comes up again, I'll be certain to avoid it'. Ultimately, 'That uphill climbing Is never through' and the pain keeps coming around.

Voice and acoustic guitars set it apart from the orchestration of the last few tracks, although a delicious string arrangement appears in the second verse. The pace is easy with a lighthearted feel, the sadness of the words bringing home the built-up despair. It ends with strings and a sense of inevitable disappointment.

'I've Had It' (Mann) (4:42)

A vivid scene is set through a relaxed way with the words, like an informal conversation. A band on the road goes through the motions of nowhere gigs to small crowds, finally grinding to a halt. It's a hauntingly autobiographical memory of a showcase gig in New York and the resulting ambivalence about live performing and the music business in general (the 'Boo' in the song being Michael Hausman).

There's a sense of finality in 'And a chance is all that I need, And I've had it', suggesting that opportunity has now gone and it's all over. 'For when things are really great, It just means everything's in its place', so it doesn't take much for something to go wrong, spoil the magic and bring everything to a crashing halt. However, the continuance of a situation can be just as damaging. If it isn't doing anyone any good, it would probably be best for it to just stop: 'I guess this is our prime, Like they tell us all the time. Weren't you expecting some other kind?'.

The 'clip-clop' rhythm with easy piano and guitar, sets up the vocals, initially from Aimee, then doubled by Brion in harmony. Warm and evocative, you can't help but be drawn in. Organ chords and percussion widen the musical vista, piano growing in strength with guitar pitching in to accentuate. The arrangement is superb, particularly when strings and woodwind appear. The guitar becomes more intense, ending wistfully on Aimee's melodious wordless phrasing, strings and percussion. A very subtle and rewarding song, it featured in Nick Hornby's book, *31 Songs*.

'Way Back When' (Mann) (4:05)

The album's last track starts by acknowledging that fact, after another Beatle-esque flourish. But it's actually a couple signing divorce papers, having reached the end of the road. It's sad, but they still appear to be on reasonable terms and remember better days with fondness. They just grew apart over time as a lot of couples do. You take your eye off the ball and before you know it, you hit the buffers.

Time came, and disappeared
No one steered and it got weirder
Help was needed, no one volunteered

There are some lovely couplets, like 'What made me think that I could weather it? You're down before you even know that you've been hit'. It ends with a sad 'Wonder if we'll ever meet again?'.

The Beatles feel bubbles under the surface, giving an upbeat *Sgt. Pepper* vibe, somewhat 'A Day In The Life' at times, in contrast to the sadness of the scenario. There's trombone from Randy Brion, barrelhouse piano adding to the surrealist edge, becoming more sophisticated, before reverting to type for the barroom lines that tie everything up. A very satisfying end to what is a superb album.

'Nothing' (Mann) (0:09)
But it's not the end! Bide your time for the best part of half a minute of silence and you're 'rewarded' with this unnecessary payoff. It probably seemed like a good idea at the time, but particularly after the unusual and fitting conclusion to the previous track, the nine seconds of annoying keyboard noise is completely superfluous.

Related Tracks
'Take It Back' (Brion, Mann) (2:52)
An 'I Should've Known' B-side (which did not feature on the expanded *Whatever*). It's an up-tempo, semi-acoustic jangle with a Byrdsian sound, toe-tapping chorus and good harmony vocals. The keyboard solo take on the main melody line is a bit cheesy but, overall, it's a good (if slightly inconsequential) song, delivered well.

Aimee is in feisty form, taking back control. In the first verse, she is reconciling her possibly derogatory thoughts regarding a partner:

Tell me your thoughts so I can
Love you in spite of them
But now I'm happy if I
Never lose sight of them

The chorus seems to underline her indecision ('And that's a fact – as of a month ago'), but there's a sense of positivity ahead, albeit tempered by 'Now that the worst is over'. She appears to be in a transient space where lovers come and go, aware that 'I'm getting better when I annex myself from you, It oughta be another country I'm moving to'.

'Baby Blue' (Pete Ham) (3:51)

This cover of Badfinger's 1972 US Top 20 hit appeared as a B-side on Aimee's first three solo singles. It can also be found on the *Exclusive Collection* and 1996's *Come and Get It: A Tribute to Badfinger*, Aimee having originally played it live in 1990.

Imago became concerned about releasing the album with no obvious single prospects, and it was requested that she write a crossover hit. Mann replied that she couldn't and ultimately recorded the Badfinger cover to try and coax in potential listeners. But she was unhappy with the results and it didn't make the album. This search for a last-minute hit resulted in the already delayed album being put back a couple more months.

It arrives with a strident fanfare of guitars, set against the plaintive voice. The hard-edged delivery and often clashing guitar lines carry it through in a production that makes it sound bigger than the original. It's a lovely song of regret, and it's nice to see Pete Ham and Badfinger getting some love.

'Jimmy Hoffa Jokes' (Mann) (2:30)

A B-side from 'Say Anything', 'I Should've Known', and later, 'That's Just What You Are' from *I'm With Stupid*, plus the *Exclusive Collection* of *Whatever*.

Stately and engaging, Aimee's voice is supported by acoustic guitar and elegiac organ, with piano adding colour. It's one of her most beautiful songs, a sorrowful shroud underlining the hopelessness of a couple who are creaking towards the end of the line, going through the motions:

> No, we're old and sad and bored
> And we're not funny anymore
> We're like Jimmy Hoffa jokes

The reference is to union boss and organised crime lynchpin, Hoffa, who disappeared in 1975.

> He's infinitely wise
> But he infinitely lies
>
> We're barely worth the wait
> We're just slightly out of date

'Truth On My Side' (Mann) (4:21)

B-side of the European release of 'I Should've Known' and included in the *Exclusive Collection*, this is a demo dating from 1989. It sounds a little thin, but it's a pleasant song – basic drums with bass, guitar and organ. It's pleasingly mid-tempo with a nice guitar solo, presumably from Jon Brion.

There are recriminations afoot and venom in the words as Aimee takes someone to task – 'Was it getting on your nerves just knowing I'm around? ... It's never enough for you to merely be unkind' – but with the belief that 'I have got the truth on my side, And that's the one thing you can't abide'.

> Some people are just stupid
> As you thought they were
> Including of course
> The ones you were rest assured would never make a stand

> You better pray that the lies you have going
> Can keep you from owing much more than you do
> 'Cause the debt just gets bigger

'Put On Some Speed' (Mann, Brion) (4:00)

Another 1989 demo, included on the *Exclusive Collection*. Unlike the title, there's no speed involved. It's laid-back and acoustic with a country feel and nice backing vocals. It's sparse, and all the better for that, with good use of piccolo. Very different from *Whatever*, as a virtual stand-alone piece, it's an easy and relaxing listen.

It seems to be an aching appeal to yourself to quit standing there saying 'C'mon, do your worst!' and 'Put on some speed', as the chorus confirms:

> No one is running for help
> 'Cause no one saves you from yourself
> You've got solutions you need

The third verse points an accusatory finger with 'You never knew me at all, Now you tell me who's at fault', as 'There's not a 'they' who's gonna stop it'.

I'm With Stupid (1995)

Personnel:
Aimee Mann: Vocals, Bass Guitar, Acoustic and Electric Guitar, Handclaps
Jon Brion: Bass Guitar, Harmonica, Cello, Drums and Percussion, Acoustic and Electric Guitar, Handclaps, Keyboards, Background Vocals
Bernard Butler: Electric Guitar, Keyboards
Mike Denneen: Keyboards
Chris Difford, Neil Innes and Juliana Hatfield: Background Vocals
Brad Hallan: Bass Guitar
Stacy Jones: Bass Guitar, Drums, Acoustic Guitar
Peter Linton, Clayton Scoble and Glenn Tilbrook: Electric Guitar, Background Vocals
Michael Lockwood: Electric Guitar
Jon Lupfer: Handclaps, Tenor Sax
Michael Penn: Acoustic Guitar
John Sands: Drums
Martyn Watson: Drum Loops
Producers: Jon Brion, Mike Denneen
Record Label: Geffen
Recorded: Q Division (Boston); Grandmaster (L.A.); Baron Jive (L.A.); The Strongroom (London); Konk (London)
Released: 11 November 1995
Running Time: 56:21
Highest chart place: US:82, UK:51

Whilst *I'm With Stupid* was coming together, lead single 'That's Just What You Are' was getting TV exposure on the soundtrack of *Melrose Place*. But Aimee was embroiled in the collapse of Imago, and it seemed that label problems would once more scupper her progress. She signed a contract with Reprise Records, but Imago prevented her from releasing any material, and for most of 1995, she battled Imago's owner Terry Ellis in an attempt to free herself. 'It's so frustrating. My album has sat around unreleased for the last three months and even if Terry cut a deal, it would take another three months to set up the release.' Asked why she didn't just leave like labelmate Henry Rollins (who later sued Imago for 'fraud, deceit, undue influence and economic coercion'), she pointed out that her contract was directly with Ellis, rather than Imago itself. 'I'm signed to a man, not a label. You think in any field, when your company goes out of business, you're allowed to look for another job. But it didn't work like that.' She talked about giving up on the music business altogether but eventually won her independence at the end of 1995.

The album was finally picked up by Geffen when they absorbed Imago's roster, and released it on the DGC Records imprint, without fanfare, in November 1995 in the UK. An American release followed in January 1996. Geffen later became part of Interscope, the scale and size of which put pressure on many smaller artists. Although happy to get the album on the shelves, Aimee confirmed to *The Albuquerque Journal* that she 'could have made a better deal with Geffen on my own if I didn't have an intermediary'.

Regarding the title of the record, as well as being an ironic take on the popular t-shirt slogan of the time, it 'sums up a certain amount of frustration I've felt in working with people whom I personally considered stupid. All I want to do is something good. It doesn't seem like asking that much. In songs where I allude to record company troubles, you're right if you think I'm plenty pissed off'. By February, she was telling *Rolling Stone* that if she had to name the album, then it would be called '*I Have Pummeled Stupid to Death in the Parking Lot*'.

Whilst her songs so often describe dysfunctional relationships – personal or business – they may not always be based on her own experiences, sometimes commenting on 'friends who have had disagreements with the industry. I've been able to observe a lot of that kind of thing these past few years'. Regarding the album's basic premise, she told *Pulse!* magazine 'It's like this: "You're a nightmare, I'm not going to get involved with you, so go away"'.

The music on *I'm With Stupid* is stripped back from the sound of *Whatever*, tougher and notably more guitar-orientated. This is a rock record, but with a light and playful touch, Jon Brion again on hand and featuring prominently. It's a reaction to *Whatever* as Aimee 'felt like there was a little too much going on throughout the first record'. If anything, there's more of a 'British' vibe than previously, reflected in her affinity for UK artists. She lived in London for most of 1994, writing with Suede's Bernard Butler, and Squeeze's Chris Difford and Glenn Tilbrook, who she also toured with. 'England has a vibe that demands that you be more creative. I spent a lot of time just hanging out and listening to music. I remembered what it was like to be so naive, it's charming.'

Aimee cited albums by Liz Phair and Beck as recent influences, 'helping me realise that every song does not have to be this elaborate construction – that sometimes very simple songs or very short songs are equally enjoyable'. Considering the album overall, 'It's definitely true that there's a more specific kind of sound on this one', She told *Pulse!*. 'If you listen to *Whatever*, you can hear what we were trying to sound like on every song: This is the Badfinger song; this is the Simon and Garfunkel song; this is the Randy Newman song. I wanted the new album to be more straightforward and to have more guitar because I'd written most of the songs on electric guitar and because I'm way crankier'.

The inroads made by 'That's Just What You Are' ahead of the album, were lost, and upon release, *I'm With Stupid* became another commercial disappointment, peaking at number 82. Amid the modest sales, Mann was still seen as a 1980s pop casualty. But the critics were still on her side and there was much praise, *Time* regarding *I'm With Stupid* as one of the 'catchiest pop albums of the year, brimming with poised three-minute mini-masterpieces. Mann has the same skill that great tunesmiths like McCartney and Neil Young have: the knack for writing simple, beautiful, instantly engaging songs. Bitterness, regret, and recrimination never sounded any sweeter, or smarter'.

When asked, after her recent travails, if she was hopeful for the future, she replied, 'Yeah, and extremely cynical at the same time. People sometimes ask if I'm bitter, and I always say "Yes, of course". But what does that mean? It means that I don't want to keep making the same mistakes and beating my head against a brick wall'. Concerning whether her career was back on the right path, she replied to *The Boston Globe* in 1996, 'This is Plan B. It's an interesting road to go down, but I don't feel like I'm back on track. I realise there is no track anymore'.

The album cover features multi-coloured magnets spelling out the title, while Aimee peers into a fridge. The reverse shows a blurred image of Aimee holding a doll. The CD inlay lists all the words used in the album's lyrics alphabetically, with one word per column highlighted in bold. Art direction was again by Gail Marowitz.

'Long Shot' (Mann) (3:13)
Right out of the blocks, Aimee pulls no punches. 'You fucked it up, you should have quit, 'til circumstances, Had changed a bit'. But what could have been the cause? 'Out of the blue, a guy I was working with made a declaration of love. Oh great. He takes our friendship, adds this twist that will always be in the air, and now we might not be able to go back to our working relationship. If he had just kept it to himself, everything would've been fine.' The 'passion paradox', that the more you like someone, the less they like you back, coming into play in 'And all that stuff, I knew before, Just turned into, 'Please love me more''.

The forceful use of the expletive three times during the song might have marked it out as a strange choice for the album's second single. She explained in a Geffen press release at the time: 'We had to do a clean version for radio, which is ridiculous because you get the *f* and *ck* and the *ed*. There really should be a context consideration. To say "You fucked it up" is different contextually from saying "I fucked him in the back seat".' Perhaps oddly, the song also appeared on a promo single as B-side to Coolio's 'Gangsta's Paradise'.

From the strange count in of 'Five, six, seven, fifty!', scratching guitar picks up the rhythm with a dancy drum pattern. The introduction of bass pushes it forward in the third verse, additional guitar embellishments from Michael Lockwood and Jon Brion filling out the basic setup. The bounce of much of *I'm With Stupid* is present from the start, and this is a fun song about an embarrassing interlude. Although they don't appear here, Difford and Tilbrook authorised the use of their riff from Squeeze's 'Up the Junction'.

'Choice In The Matter' (Brion, Mann) (3:13)
With backing vocals from Glenn Tilbrook (and a little bit of Chris Difford), it's another simple song that Aimee confirmed is about 'being in someone's apartment and their answering machine is full of messages, but they won't play

them back while you're there.' The underlying tone of secrets and deception immediately puts the singer on guard to a potential concern – he's giving her no choice but to avoid getting involved with him. 'Skip the cloak and dagger bit', she says as she foresees a situation of 'Ignorance without the bliss'. There's awareness of the futility of going on in 'Cause I know where this boat will go, Pulled down by the undertow, It's lucky I know how to row', followed by a chorus of 'Row, row, row your boat' (ending with the darkly sinister 'I hope you drown and never come back').

The rough and driving sound of the basic band setup is prominent throughout. Brion's solos are confident, the rockier sound clearly suiting Aimee, her voice coolly set against the backdrop. A live version was a B-side for 'You Could Make A Killing'.

A movie sound clip opens the song. I haven't found the source, but it sets up the scene nicely. 'And if this is one of your ten-thousand-dollar hours, Don't forget to write it down, Help is on the way'.

'Sugarcoated' (Bernard Butler, Mann) (3:39)

Aimee confirmed that this is about co-writer Bernard Butler. 'He'd left Suede, and the press was intimating that he was some spoiled rock star. And you meet him and he's the sweetest guy. But everyone else gets sugarcoated and he comes out looking like the bad guy.' 'Sugarcoated, When they wrote it, I would've believed it too'. She was I London and heard that Butler wanted to work with other people. 'I called him up. We wrote a song and Jon (Brion) was with us – there's your drummer and there's your second guitarist. So we recorded it. The whole thing took two days.'

Emerging from feedback, Butler's guitar is immediately prominent. There's a freewheeling feel in his distinctive and unrestrained soloing, building to the bridge:

> And out of your mouth
> Comes a stream of cliches
> Now I have given you so much rope
> You should have been hanging for days
> But you keep spinning it out

Butler then launches into a swooping section. The intensity steps back in the final verse, roaring in once more with 'Now I'm the Antichrist'. Keyboard additions colour the rest, with another distinctive Butler passage to close. It's a satisfying song that benefits greatly from his involvement, underlining the rockier nature of the album.

'You Could Make A Killing' (Mann) (3:21)

Noel Gallagher of Oasis is the inspiration here; 'His desire to be somebody, his drive to be successful. When you have such a drive, that feeling can be very strong. But sometimes when you make that killing, you don't realise what you've left behind, what you've missed on the way. People get fixed on a certain thing and they just have to have it at all costs. As a bystander, you're likely to get trampled underfoot. It's not even that big a deal, it's just a habit. It's the habit that will trample you'.

There's a sharp sarcasm in 'I wish I was both young and stupid, Then I too could have the fun that you did', noting the juvenile goings-on within Oasis, coupling unworldliness with a lack of consideration for others. 'I could follow you and search the rubble, Or stay right here and save myself some trouble'.

The setup remains basic, Aimee and Jon playing all the instruments, with Juliana Hatfield adding high harmonies. 'I don't sing really high, so Juliana was perfect. She's got that kid thing, I love that. I have this vibrato that I can't really get rid of and she has absolutely none.' From tinkling bell effects, Aimee counts in a folky acoustic sound, although with distorted electric guitar. It makes a nice contrast to the previous songs, Aimee disguising the pointed words in plaintive tones.

'Superball' (Mann) (3:05)

'You're a million places at once. With a superball, one little throw and the thing never stops. It's like, "Don't get me started, you have no idea what you're getting into."' This boundless energy can be disruptive and damaging:

> And I warn you now
> The velocity I'm gathering
> Will knock you down
> Send the chairs and lamps all scattering

The almost pitiful payoff 'It's got nothing to do with me' confirms that it's nature rather than conscious decision-making.

Fun and upbeat, a dense sound with distorted guitars skims off the walls in superball style. The rhythm is steady with elasticity in the bass. But this is all about Brion's guitar, including a nice descending solo, reprised at the end with handclaps, culminating in an unexpected scratchy blues sample.

'Amateur' (Brion, Mann) (4:51)

Aimee noted in a 2007 ASCAP interview how Jon would often start a song and 'just hand me a little chord progression and some words and melody, or some kernel of an idea. And I just always found his music very inspiring, so it was very easy for me to make a whole song out of that. He would always tell me right away what the concept of the lyric was and I'd always know immediately what he was talking about'.

'Amateur' was such a song. Aimee and Jon had been in a three-year romance and he wrote it about their breakup. Despite the potentially upsetting content, Aimee wrote the lyric based on his concept. 'His plot instructions were:

"When you and I broke up and we were trying to get back together and all my friends were saying, 'Why would you go back to that nightmare? ' this song would be your answer to them'". The use of the word 'amateur' suggests that although things were done for love, a lack of worldliness and guile meant that it never turned out as hoped. 'This was his explanation of why he wanted to keep trying. Even though I'm the villain, it's just about understanding what happened.'

From the 'olde worlde' acoustic waltz of brushed drums and piano, the pace and tone is mature as the lyric dissects the fall-out, the singer confirming that, in love, her ex was an amateur. 'I was hoping that you'd know better, But I've been wrong before.' There's a touch of Burt Bacharach moving beautifully through the verses. Brion adds an affecting solo, supported by strings and tinged with sadness, the lazy feel completing via an extended outro. It's one of the key moments of the album and one of Aimee's finest songs. The video features flickering black and white footage, moving through city scenes in winter, eventually finding Aimee in the studio, intercut with live footage – melancholy and a good fit for the song.

'All Over Now' (Mann) (3:37)

This is about 'someone who tries to be very controlling and goes way too far, tightens their grip and ends up losing their grip on reality'. The lyric shows her discomfort as an 'Inch became a light-year, It was pathetic'. She's aware of the control ('Must you leave your fingerprints on everything I called mine?') and isn't prepared to put up with it:

Oh you can write the play
And every word I say
But I don't have to stay
To see the credits

Anger crackles as she describes the interference which took hold of her life, her lack of say, focused in the repeated 'It's got nothing to do with me'. But the last lines are a warning to back off, the chorus confirming an ultimately positive outcome with 'It's all over now, and I'm free'.

A strong drum rhythm kicks in, Bernard Butler back to spray some fine guitar over it, although the solos go to Jon Brion, Peter Linton, and finally, Aimee. Pain and frustration shine out from this guitar-heavy anthem-to-independence. There's a lovely swing, the varying guitar styles making for an interesting listen.

'Par For The Course' (Mann) (6:01)

'I saw a friend of mine getting into a situation where he was just going to get his heart broken into a million pieces. Mr Pattern Guy. It's happened before and it'll happen again. You're not even in the situation, but you know it's all gonna end in tears.'

The 'par for the course' result is that 'You bet the wrong horse'. You sense the despair as the object of the song cries in self-pity for the loss of a love he wants but ultimately can't have. There's an almost callous 'It's all you deserve'. She's been there before and can't sugar the pill for him. 'The loss of the nerve, The grade of the curve' caused him to lose out as 'She swerved out of your path'. Her own bitterness for lost opportunities shines through as she notes that 'Timing is everything in this game, So let's have a moment of blame'.

Unusually, Aimee plays and sings everything here, with the intimate atmosphere you'd expect as a result. At six minutes, it's long, but it carries itself beautifully throughout. The words come straight in over strident acoustic chords, a subdued rhythm and electric guitar taking over towards the end of the verse, getting grittier into the chorus. There's almost a country feel; emotion wrung out of the words as it builds at a funereal pace and she declaims 'I don't even know you anymore', repeated and probably directed at herself as much as him. The intensity relieves for the final verse of voice and chorded guitar, building again with keyboard strings and an electric solo. A very powerful piece.

Aimee has admitted to being particularly proud of this song. 'There's a whole feeling of resignation about the lyrics that the music makes you feel. I remember when Jon and I would work on that song, everybody's blood pressure would drop, and you could barely find a pulse in the studio. It would always have to be the last thing we worked on in the day because it had a physically depressing effect.'

'You're With Stupid Now' (Mann) (3:27)

It's 'kind of about my past record company situation and kind of about a big fan of mine – I have the most bizarre fans – who's a politician in England. He's very dedicated and altruistic. He really tries to do good work and change things and is always frustrated'.

Aimee whispers in your ear on the right channel, the first verse suggesting a 'tug of war' label fight with words directed at herself in a plaintive 'Though you'd rather that they just ignore you'. The 'Stupid' of the title could be construed as being either party.

The politician friend was the late British Labour MP, Tony Banks (who helped her during her struggle with Imago), the second verse 'tilting at windmills' element shining through, with an appearance by 'the crazy will of Margaret Thatcher', as possessed by his opponents. The futility of trying to do what you perceive to be right against overwhelming odds, is beautifully captured in 'You don't know how to manufacture, Sturdy bones with a hairline fracture'. There's handshaking and speeches and mistakes made as those around him 'struggle with the undertaking of simple thought' – a damning indictment of the realities of political life. 'What you want you don't know'. Again, the 'Stupid' could be those around him, or ironically the politician himself, the song ending with a world-weary 'So on with the show'.

Recorded as a duo piece with Brion, it's acoustic guitars to start, with electric accents, low-key and calm, with Brion supporting the vocal in the chorus. Acoustic bass comes in for the second verse and there's a lovely warmth, Brion adding a sparse solo that captures the song's mood before the repetition of the final chorus.

'That's Just What You Are' (Brion, Mann) (4:22)

Appearing ahead of the album in 1994, Aimee confirmed that she was in England at the time and had planned to release the song as a stand-alone single when the *Melrose Place* soundtrack opportunity appeared. Disappointingly, when it was finally released in 1995, it only reached number 93 in *Billboard*.

Aimee has noted the song as a response to Jon Brion, telling a friend that 'he'd frequently behaved in an appalling fashion, but the friend said that to change would compromise his personality. He was using "Hey, I am just what I am" to justify acting like a jerk'. She also confirmed that this was another song which Brion had started, before she came in to write the bridge and finish it off.

The lyric is to the point: 'Don't sit there and think you're off of the hook by saying there is no use changing 'cause that's just what you are'.

Acting steady always ready to defend your fears
What's the matter with the truth, did I offend your ears
By suggesting that a change might be a thing to try
Like it would kill you just to try and be a nicer guy

Drum loops colour this one, Difford and Tilbrook appearing again, the latter adding the guitar solo. Mike Denneen gets a brief organ solo and the feel is generally upbeat, vocals swapping between singers and between channels toward the end.

The video is unusual, Aimee spray-painting objects in the desert (which is revealed to be a stage set), with multiple costume changes (including a tartan suit) amid stop-motion elements. An acoustic version appeared as B-side of the 'Long Shot' single.

'Frankenstein' (Brion, Mann) (4:25)

Aimee told *The Richmond Times*, 'The best part of a relationship for most people is when it's just beginning, and they can make this person in their own mind into this creature that doesn't exist. The other person becomes this construction of desires and fears and aspirations and ways that you want to be treated, or ways that you're afraid you're going to be treated'.

The song starts with the realisation that 'I don't know you from Adam'. He's a fantasy that's probably better than the reality. 'When you're building your own creation, Nothing's better than real than a real imitation'. There's reference to 'Chekhov's Gun', a theatrical device named for Anton Chekhov whose advice to writers stated, 'If in the first act you have hung a pistol on the wall, then in the following one it should be fired. Otherwise don't put it there'. This was lyrically acknowledged with 'When the gun in the first act goes off in the third'. The unexpected is always likely to happen in this kind of manufactured relationship. After all, 'It's rare that you ever know what to expect, From a guy made of corpses with bolts in his neck'.

'And you'll notice it bears a resemblance to, Everything I imagined I wanted from you'. In the end, however, it's just a pointless exercise:

> And when later we find that the thing we devised
> Has the villagers clamouring for its demise
> We will have to admit the futility of
> Trying to make something more of this jerry-built love

There could also be an autobiographical aside on how Mann's fame has hampered her in forming relationships, as 'The most perfect strangers that you can talk to, are the ones who pretend that you're not really you'.

The concept of creating a structure from bits and pieces, followed through into the recording:

> I was writing it in the studio when Jon was working on something else, and I told him what it was about. So I hear him go into the storage room and he's got a stick in his hand and he's just hitting things. Forty-five minutes later I go to tell him that I've finished the song, and sitting in the studio is this drum kit he's pieced together out of joint compound boxes and ashtrays where when you hit the stand, it rings in tune with the song. This other box of bolts was the snare. Of course, I said, 'That's all very cute Jon, but does it sound good?'. And it sounded perfect. It was not only sonically ideal for the song, but it had the concept of the song in it.

Brion is largely responsible for the instrumentation. It starts with another film soundtrack clip, most likely from one of the *Frankenstein* movies: 'I still have the shake in my voice, And I'm going to sing you this song'. From there, the unorthodox percussion makes its presence felt, clanky, and suiting the upbeat, mid-paced DIY feel. The guitars become more strident toward the end, including a wonky solo, with quirky keyboards and old-style cinema organ. An unusual song, but it works.

'Ray' (Mann) (4:47)

'My love song to my imaginary friend, to a person you've never met and probably never will. Sometimes you need to write a love song, and so what if there's nobody there? You have to invent somebody, an imaginary friend for grown-ups.'

Like 'Frankenstein', It's an amalgam of different individuals to create 'your ideal person. Kind of the way I'd feel about someone if they weren't such a total nightmare'.

Despite being imaginary, where everything could be just wonderful, 'Ray' starts acoustically with a hint of regret in the lines 'As of today, I can't say things will ever be the same, And that could be a shame.' Ray is referenced as 'another lonely exile' and 'as bad off as me', so the hope is that these two lost souls can heal each other's pain. 'Can we repay ourselves for days that we've lost through indecision, With one of recognition?' There's a gentle yearning in this quest for 'some you just believe in, And hope it comes out even'.

Harmonium (by Jon Brion, credited as 'Ringo') adds a distinctive texture, drums crashing in to lift the pace, a lovely upright piano flavour coming through. There's again an element of homemade to the percussion. A heartfelt piece, even if it is aimed at a figment of her imagination.

'It's Not Safe' (Mann) (5:02)

This appears to consider Mann's impending move to record label independence, and she confirmed that:

> (It is) completely, 100 per cent about feeling that professionally you're involved with people who don't understand what you're doing, don't care what you're doing, and thwart your every move. And because it's of such a personal nature, you just question the whole process. You wonder, 'Why am I doing this, why bother?'. I hadn't written for a long time before I wrote that song. I felt like I didn't want to tell these people anything. I didn't want to give anything away.

You'd better keep your thoughts to yourself, ''Cause God knows it's not safe with anybody else'.

> All you want to do is something good
> So get ready to be ridiculed and misunderstood
> 'Cause don't you know that you're a fucking freak in this world
> In which everybody's willing to choose swine over pearls

Stick to your guns and try again, 'But a thousand compromises don't add up to a win' and your handlers will 'be happy if you'd only cover your tracks' and repeat a formula that has already proven successful.

There's despair in 'So maybe everything is all for nothing', as the song describes an 'idiot who keeps believing in luck'. (Followed by 'And you just can't get it through your head that no one else gives a fuck'). Aimee acknowledges her own idiocy. 'In this business, people often say one thing and do another', she told *The Performing Artist* in 1999, 'and for a long time, I guess I did believe, until I finally reached the point where I stopped believing and just got out'.

By 2007, she seemed to have put the matter to bed and stopped letting it get to her:

I'm now satisfied that I can't do anything to make it better, I just equate it with anybody who's ever had to get out of a bad relationship. Believe in luck? Sure, you can be like Annie, you know, the sun will come out tomorrow, but that's crazy. I'd rather be perky and optimistic on my own behalf, and whatever happens, happens.

Glenn Tilbrook's backing vocals appear, alongside a perhaps unexpected Neil Innes of The Bonzo Dog Doo-Dah Band, and The Rutles. There's a jangly 1960s feel and a Beatles influence that adds another facet to the album. But the guitars still rule, Michael Penn contributing the dignified and tasteful solos. A fine way to end the album. Or is it...?

Related Tracks
Untitled Hidden Track (Mann) (1:21)
The US version has a brief additional track, separated from the main album by 53 seconds of silence. It's a lovely bit of fun, starting with 'Play that guitar', a twangy solo, birdsong, and a Beatles pastiche (likely to be Innes) in the line 'But you're the idiot who keeps believing in luck', before a big band jazz interlude. Finally, a distorted voice delivers the coda:

> The speaker is out of the picture
> I'm talking to the microphone
> The microphone thinks that I'm talking
> But I'm not talking at all
> I'm singing to you

'Driving With One Hand On The Wheel' (Mann) (2:44)
B-side of the UK 'Long Shot' single, it also appeared on the 1996 compilation *Safe and Sound: A Benefit in Response to the Brookline Clinic Violence*, released in the wake of an anti-abortion attack in Massacusetts on 30 December 1994 that left receptionists Shannon Lowney and Lee Ann Nichols dead and five others wounded.

After the count-in, the instrumentation is sparse as Aimee sings happily (if ironically):

> You asked me to dinner
> You brought me stuff
> Now what do I make of that
> You made me an offer
> I called your bluff
> Now you're an amnesiac

The chorus, 'Driving with one hand on the wheel, Ordering luck with every meal, Feeding on hope again never mind how small a portion' looks for positivity in the situation, but with an awareness that it's likely to be in short supply.

The full band kick in for the second verse, with the lovely couplet 'And who would've thought that initial drink, Would clear an entire shelf'. The bridge adds keyboard lines to get to the heart of the matter. 'You should look at it realistically, I know you couldn't be in love with me'. The third verse calls out his 'hoping for the best' attitude, and the resulting 'appalling mess', before slowing into the coda. Overall, a fun and musically upbeat song with a bouncing melody.

'Nobody Does It Better' (Marvin Hamlisch, Carole Bayer Sager) (4:26)

An intriguing 1997 cover of the theme song to the 1977 James Bond film *The Spy Who Loved Me*, originally sung by Carly Simon, here reimagined for David Arnold's *Shaken and Stirred* Bond tribute. Starting with harmonium, in Aimee's own style, it soon morphs into typical Arnold, with programmed drums and big production. It's certainly different and worth hearing.

Magnolia – Original Soundtrack (1999)

Personnel (Aimee Mann tracks):
Aimee Mann: Vocals, Acoustic Guitar, Bass
Jon Brion: Acoustic and Electric Guitars, Bass, Keyboards, Melodica, Chamberlin, Celeste, Drums and Percussion, Backing Vocals
Michael Lockwood: Acoustic, Electric and 12-string Guitars, Keyboards, Melodica, Backing Vocals
Patrick Warren: Piano, Keyboards, Chamberlin, Celeste, Accordion
Buddy Judge: Acoustic Guitar, Backing Vocals
Dan MacCarroll, Scott Mitchell, Rick Menck, John Sands: Drums and Percussion
Brendan O'Brien: Slide Guitar, Bass
Keith Brion: Piccolo
Randy Brion: Euphonium
Mike Breaux: Oboe
Jon Lupfer: Baritone Sax
Michael Hausman: Drum Programming
Benmont Tench: Piano, Chamberlin
Michael Penn: Electric Guitar, Backing Vocals
Neil Innes, Chris Difford, Juliana Hatfield: Backing Vocals
Producers: Jon Brion, Buddy Judge, Aimee Mann, Brendan O'Brien, Michael Penn
Record Label: Warner Music
Recorded: Q Division, Konk Studios, Bearsville, MixThis!, Mad Dog Studios, Audities
Released: 7 December 1999
Running Time: 50:49
Highest chart place: US:58, UK: –

In 1998, Aimee made her first movie appearance, in the Coen Brothers' *The Big Lebowski,* playing a German nihilist who sacrifices her green nail-polished pinky toe as part of a kidnapping plot. It includes a diner scene where she orders lingonberry pancakes in German! In 2012 she said, 'I really can't act, it's madness to have me in the movie. But my goal is to do better at acting than most actors have done at singing'.

Filmmaker, Paul Thomas Anderson (who had success in 1997 with *Boogie Nights*) used her songs as an inspiration for characters and situations in his third film, *Magnolia*, likening the experience to sharing his 'personal Aimee Mann mixtape'. Aimee was now married to Michael Penn and living in Los Angeles. Regarding her meeting with Anderson, she recalled, 'Paul contacted Michael first to score his movie *Hard Eight* (1996, Anderson's debut feature) and they became friends, and then that's how I got to know Paul. Then I think we introduced him to the Largo (comedy club) scene, where he met Jon Brion and started working with Jon'. Mann and Anderson bonded immediately, as both experienced problems with commercially focused studios and industry players, Anderson saying, 'It made me very gun-shy, anxious to be in total control'.

The finished film is populated by characters who could easily feature in Mann's songs. Strange and emotionally fragile, with flawed personalities and a history of traumatic life experiences, the fractured nature of their lives was laid bare. A number of the songs used were previously written, but Aimee wrote several specifically for the project, also recording a cover of Harry Nilsson's 'One'. The soundtrack also features songs performed by Supertramp and Gabrielle. Jon Brion wrote the orchestral score, which was released separately, one piece appearing on this 'songs' collection. The opening of 'You Could Make A Killing', and the untitled hidden track from the end of *I'm With Stupid*, appear briefly at the start of the film but didn't make the album.

Many of the songs feature prominently in the film, which weaves nine distinct yet connected storylines happening on a single day in California's San Fernando Valley. In Anderson's words, it's 'a *fuck-you* celebration of the Valley', with an ensemble cast featuring Tom Cruise, Julianne Moore, Philip Seymour Hoffman, William H Macy, John C Reilly and Jason Robards.

Anderson 'sat down to write an adaptation of Aimee Mann songs', confirming to *The Guardian*, 'I had her two solo albums and a lot of her demos, because she's a friend, and I think the tone she gets is really beautiful. So I thought about using them as a basis, or as inspiration for the film'. His script started as lists of interesting things; 'Images, words, ideas, and slowly they start resolving themselves into sequences and shots and dialogue'.

Mann is certainly integral to the film: a character snorts cocaine off one of her CDs, another directly quotes a song lyric. A montage of the entire cast singing 'Wise Up' also features, to spellbinding effect. Anderson had already received recognition for his song choices for *Boogie Nights*, and Aimee noted to *Interview* magazine in 2009 his 'ability to step back and allow the music to take over and tell the story in a different way, in an emotional way that hits you in a different place'. She acknowledged to *The Gaurdian* Anderson's comment that characters were written based on people she was talking about in her songs. 'But it's also his interpretation and his writing, so you know, it's heavily coloured by him. I wouldn't say if I were to put my songs into movie form, it would come out exactly the same way.'

Commercially, the soundtrack sold well, particularly in the US where it went gold, and was nominated for three Grammys: Best Soundtrack, Best Song Written for Visual Media and Best Female Pop Vocal Performance.

'One' (Harry Nilsson) (2:53)

Played during the film's opening sequence, introducing the various characters, this cover of Harry Nilsson's 1968 song (made famous by Three Dog Night in 1969) moves away from the string-based original and adds guitars. It keeps a lot of the keyboard parts in a more elaborate arrangement, but otherwise, it's played pretty straight and retains the haunting delicacy. Aimee originally recorded it for the 1995 tribute album, *For the Love of Harry: Everybody Sings Nilsson*.

The opening line, 'One is the loneliest number that you'll ever do', perfectly sets out the yearning sense of loss in *Magnolia*, compounded by 'Two can be as bad as one, It's the loneliest number since the number one'. Nilsson wrote his original after getting an engaged telephone signal, the *beep beep beep* of the *busy* signal becoming the opening notes, the pulse continuing throughout.

Aimee's version contains several obscure Nilsson references. It opens with a sample of Nilsson saying 'Okay, Mr. Mix!' (from the start of his song 'Cuddly Toy'). Lyrics from Nilsson's 'Together' are sung in the background ('Life isn't easy when two are divided, And one has decided to bring down the curtain, And one thing's for certain, There's nothing to keep them together'), and the opening melodic vocal motif from his 'Good Old Desk' is also incorporated. Neil Innes and Chris Difford provide backing vocals, all the instrumentation by the inimitable Jon Brion.

'Momentum' (Mann) (3:27)

Once again, the majority of the instruments are played by Brion, with Buddy Judge's acoustic guitar, drums from Dan MacCarroll, and Jon Lupfer's baritone sax. 'Momentum' features in the film as the loud music that Claudia Wilson plays in her apartment, leading to police officer Jim Kurring's attendance after a complaint.

It's about the headlong rush through life, the pace of a career which has 'allowed my fears to get larger than life'. With that life getting shorter, the set routine is pushing any chance to change the situation, into the background. The desire for 'seizing the day' is set against the 'effort expended' and the 'minutes and days and hours I have frittered away', and there's a panic for the time now lost, which suits the torn and unstable side of Claudia's character.

The ominous piano chord and discordant opening, move into a 1930s jazz swing with brass and upright bass. It sounds confident and driving, but this masks the sadness as the words gnaw away at the soul, the final couplet: 'I'm condemning the future to death, So it can match the past' – devastatingly brutal. With Brion's wailing guitar solo as the song builds, it's upbeat with the everything-including-the-kitchen-sink arrangement of a packed existence. That's until the seemingly abrupt ending, which ebbs slowly away on a long fade of swinging drums, appended at the close by crashing, almost surf, guitar. It's unusual within Aimee's catalogue but fits the mood and context well.

'Build That Wall' (Mann, Brion) (4:25)

The use of wind and brass is expanded here, Brion sticking to guitar, percussion and keyboards while Aimee straps on her bass. There's a steady pulse, with organ, twinkling glockenspiel, and euphonium (from Randy Brion) adding a lovely tone to the easy pacing. Mike Breaux's oboe offers a hint of sadness against the lightness of piccolo (from Jon's father Keith). The sweeping orchestration fills the sound, giving an almost 1960s pop vibe, with excellent backing vocals from Jon, Aimee and Buddy Judge.

This song dates back to 1990, the lyric concerning a friend who ignores advice and reconnects with someone from her past who is bad news. She's 'Courtin' disaster in an undertone' but won't listen to reason, and builds a wall between her and those who care about her well-being. There's frustration in 'How could anyone ever fight it?, Who could ever expect to fight it?'. But once the call has been made, there's nothing more that can be done – she's made her choice, given away by her guilty face. It's time to decide whether their friendship can wait it out, or if it's time to leave it and move on ('Maybe it's one where time will tell, Maybe it's one where it's just fare thee well'). But it seems that the latter is the only option as the singer decides to 'learn to build that wall' of her own.

It's like a warm hug, intimate and beautiful, a gorgeous song of depth, all the way through to a very satisfying conclusion. Just wonderful.

'Deathly' (Mann) (5:28)

One of several *Magnolia* songs that also appeared on Aimee's next solo album, *Bachelor No.2*. In the film, a slight variation of the song's startling opening lines, 'Now that I've met you, Would you object to never seeing each other again?', is spoken by Claudia to Jim after they kiss on their first (and seemingly last) date. The song was pivotal as an inspiration for Claudia's character, Paul Thomas Anderson confirming that she emerged from that line, and he wrote backwards from there. He labels this moment 'The heart and soul of *Magnolia*', the other stories branching off from Claudia's.

The opening lines, with Aimee accompanying herself on acoustic guitar, are backed up with the damning observation that the singer 'can't afford to climb aboard you, No one's got that much ego to spend'. There's a resigned and cynical heard-it-all-before plea in 'So don't work your stuff, Because I've got troubles enough', and a warning in 'Don't pick on me, When one act of kindness could be deathly, Definitely'.

As in the film, Claudia sees herself as 'just a problem for you to solve and watch dissolve in the heat of your charm'. Jim is a good, God-fearing man. But because of her drug addiction, Claudia knows that she's 'a goner' and beyond help. She knows that he is going to try to 'fix' her, but doesn't want to bring down this person who she has feelings for – in the brutal knowledge that, eventually, the only thing he will be able to do for her, is 'be my saviour and get out the gun', to put her out of her misery.

From simple beginnings, Aimee's bass comes in with the vibrant drums. Electric guitar gradually builds, finally letting loose with a hint at Michael Lockwood's awesome soaring guitar solo. That comes out of nowhere before the third verse, taking full-flight after the last chorus. It's a mightily majestic song that starts small and ends with the stately power of the solo.

'Driving Sideways' (Mann, Michael Lockwood) (3:47)

Also appearing on Aimee's next solo album, 'Driving Sideways' is sung to a partner, the driving metaphor of the title cleverly carried through to describe a relationship that is going nowhere. He isn't as committed as he needs to be:

You took the jack
And changed the flat
And got behind the wheel
Now you're driving sideways
Taken in by the scenery

But he has to try and do it alone as she 'Will not help you to navigate, For fear she may be wrong', which suggests a domineering influence where she is unable to speak her mind. He says that they're making headway and goes faster. 'But you're mistaking speed, for getting what you need, And never even noticing, You never do arrive'. He thinks they're nearly there, 'powered by the hopeful lie that it's just around the bend'. Throughout it all, she 'sings along', thinking that he's going to handle it, 'Until you prove her wrong'.

There's an easy roll to the initial vocal with Patrick Warren's piano, the chorus much more expansive with Michael Penn and Michael Lockwood providing electric, acoustic and 12-string, with added slide from Brendan O'Brien. The pace remains easy with a country vibe, piano at hand throughout. The slide solo at the end is nicely judged, and it's a striking song of a journey that appears easier on the surface than it actually is.

'You Do' (Mann) (3:41)

A deceptively simple song, light acoustic guitars and celeste colour the opening as Aimee sings sweetly. The basic chorus is beautifully realised, a strong vocal with a lovely melodic electric guitar phrase. Aimee hits her higher range in this intimate song that could just as easily be about herself as about an acquaintance.

I tend to go for the internal monologue view; she stays at his house, despite telling herself that he's just another jerk, trading sex for what she hopes is love. 'Just another thing that he'll be careless of'. He's making it difficult by adding 'caveats galore', which means 'You've only got to love him more' if you want to keep him. 'And you do, You really do'.

She knows she has to leave him, writing a note before she does. But after 'dissecting every word he said', she foolishly concludes that 'anyone can change'.

Another that appeared on *Bachelor No.2*, 'You Do' is a hauntingly sad song about ignoring the warning signs, forming the basis of a *Magnolia* character that was cut from the finished film.

'Nothing Is Good Enough' (Mann) (3:10)

Another *Bachelor No.2* song, here in its instrumental form, so we'll discuss it later. It appears after 'Save Me', over *Magnolia*'s end credits.

'Wise Up' (Mann) (3:31)

Previously featured on the soundtrack for *Jerry Maguire* in 1996, the song was successfully stitched into *Magnolia* to become the emotional high-point of the movie, sung by the cast. Mann said to *Penny Black* in 2017, 'I think Paul (Thomas Anderson) had heard it and felt that it was a shame that it hadn't had more use gotten out of it or had more attention'. Well, it certainly does here.

In 2009, Aimee admitted to *Interview* that the first time she saw the characters singing it, 'was crazy. I couldn't imagine how that scene was going to work. I was really worried about it. It just seemed to be such an odd idea that I didn't see how it was going to make sense and not look stupid'. However, she hadn't considered Anderson's defined 'sense of the surreal. It's like his surreal is more real than real. It was surreal, but it came across as emotionally realistic'. Later, recalling the moment to *Penny Black*, she said, 'I could not picture that at all, but that just illustrates the difference between somebody who thinks visually versus somebody who works almost entirely just in words and music'. 'I wondered about that moment too,' Anderson said to *The Guardian*, 'But I tricked everyone by getting Julianne Moore to do it first. She can always set the pace, because actors are so competitive. Then everyone was up for it'.

It's a wrenchingly sad song, but its use in the context of the film is particularly striking, where it could have come across as cheesy. It powerfully ties all the disparate characters together at the end of an emotional build-up. From Benmont Tench's stark piano, Aimee's voice is bare and emotionally exposed in its simplicity. Brion's orchestral backing of Chamberlin strings is warm and supportive against the basic rhythm. The simple yet elegiac chorus is striking, with supporting vocals from Michael Penn, and the song wrings every drop of emotion until the fractured denouement, strings fading to silence.

Another song about a relationship not working out and needing to be ended. Like the worries and troubles of life eating away at us, the only solution is to make peace with them. It's interesting to look at how the song ties in with *Magnolia*'s characters and the lines they sing. Life has not been good to Claudia, she's haunted by a past which has driven her to drugs. 'It's not what you thought when you first began it, you got what you want, Now you can hardly stand it'. Her new almost-boyfriend Jim is lonely. A figure of fun amongst his fellow police officers, he realises that 'It's not going to stop, 'til you wise up'. Quiz show host Jimmy Gator is 'sure there's a cure, And you have finally found it', planning suicide to take away the pain, much of which he has brought on himself. While ageing Quiz Kid Donnie Smith's life has been ruined by his youthful success on Jimmy's show. He turns to alcohol where 'One drink will shrink you, 'til you're underground and living down'. It numbs the pain, but it's a one-way trip likely to end in your demise. Phil Parma and his terminal patient Earl Partridge almost sing an eerie duet of 'It's not going to stop' – Earl's pain only going to end one way. Earl's trophy wife Linda has realised that she really does love him and doesn't want the money she married him for, taking an overdose of his medication after disowning her interest in his will. 'Prepare a list of what you need, Before you sign away the deed'. Earl's son, Frank T. J. Mackey, has been fighting the pain of his mother's death his whole life, alienating himself from his absentee father. Frank's pain is 'not going to stop' until he reconnects with Earl.

The final lines are striking in their simplicity, honesty and truth: 'No, It's not going to stop, So just give up'. Delivered by Stanley, the current Quiz Kid, the youngest character offers the real insight, that to move on, you have to stop the behaviours in which you're currently entrenched. It's the right and most optimistic thing to do: give up the thing that's eating away at your soul, the pride, the feelings of worthlessness, the barriers, the misdirected love, the controlling influences and the lies. In Stanley's case, he rebels against being a puppet of his father's greed, the fate that ruined Donnie's life. *All* the characters need to learn from their poor choices and move on. They need to 'Wise up'.

'Save Me' (Mann) (4:35)

The song that brought Aimee's music to wider attention, via Academy Award and Golden Globe nominations. She sang it during the Oscar ceremony ('that was very surreal. I really didn't feel like I belonged there ...', she told *Variety* in 2020, 'That was just so far from my life') but lost the award for Best Original Song to Phil Collins' 'You'll Be In My Heart' from Disney's *Tarzan*. This lead to 'Save Me''s ironic dedication to Collins at live shows or its introduction as 'The song that lost an Oscar to Phil Collins and his cartoon monkey love song'. In typically self-deprecating fashion, Aimee described herself as 'Oscar loser' in her Twitter account details.

'Save Me' has similarities with 'Wise Up' but is its flipside. In 'Wise Up', there's a realisation that the way to improve things is to leave the failing relationship, to take responsibility for your own actions and change the situation, while in 'Save Me' the protagonist needs 'Peter Pan or Superman' to save them from their crushing loneliness. It's a cry of desperation, for help, to achieve the same outcome.

From strummed acoustic guitar, Aimee's vocal is sparse ('You look like a perfect fit, For a girl in need of a tourniquet'). The arrangement gradually grows to include melodica (subtly quoting The Carpenters' 'Superstar' around the three-and-a-half-minute mark) and a key contribution from Patrick Warren's accordion, including a brief solo. Aimee's bass-playing is wonderfully melodic, bouncy and sliding, adding a slinkiness to the languid and engaging melodies. The 'But can you save me...' chorus is initially fragile, yet harmonically beautiful, with the killer punch in the misery of the following lines: 'From the ranks of the freaks, Who suspect they could never love anyone'.

It becomes more strident with Lockwood's abrasive guitar solo, before returning to the elegant calm, almost a silent scream of despair, delivered in velvet warmth. Warren's solo leads into a much more refined offering from Lockwood, with sighing backing vocals. Drummer, John Sands, noted his love for this song and how recording it was just 'One take and done, some songs play themselves'.

The video was directed by Paul Thomas Anderson and features Aimee singing the song in the presence of the movie's main characters. They sit in contemplation in their own scenes as Aimee sings nearby, slightly aloof, on the outside looking in. It was included on the European version of *Bachelor No.2*.

Bachelor No.2 (Or, the Last Remains Of The Dodo) (2000)

Personnel:
Aimee Mann: Vocals, Bass, Acoustic and Electric Guitars, Percussion
Jon Brion: Drums, Electric Guitar, Keyboards, Background Vocals
Michael Hausman: Drum Programming and Percussion
Butch, Ric Menck, John Sands: Drums and Percussion
Buddy Judge: Background Vocals, Wurlitzer, Drum Loops and Programming
Michael Lockwood: Acoustic, Electric and 12-string Guitars, Keyboards,
Background Vocals
Mark Flannagan: Trumpet
Brendan O'Brien: Bass Guitar, Slide Guitar
Michael Penn: Acoustic, Electric and Slide Guitar, Feedback, Background Vocals
Juliana Hatfield, Grant Lee Phillips: Background Vocals
Clayton Scoble: Electric Baritone Guitar
Benmont Tench: Piano, Chamberlin
Jennifer Trynin: Electric Guitar
Patrick Warren: Piano, Accordion, Celeste, Keyboards, Chamberlin
Hank Linderman: Drum Programming
Producers: Jon Brion, Mike Denneen, Buddy Judge, Aimee Mann, Brendan O'Brien
Record Label: SuperEgo, V2
Recorded: Mad Dog, Sound Chamber, Q Division, Hook, Aimee's House, Bobby
Wood's House
Released: 2 May 2000
Running Time: 49:21
Highest chart place: US:134, UK:3

The songs for her next album were deemed unsuitable by Interscope (with whom she was now signed after their merger with Geffen) due to lack of commercial appeal, causing her to give up on the majors entirely. After much argument and persistence, and as a result of the success of *Magnolia*, she again managed to get out of her contract. But there was pressure against her retaining her masters, which she eventually managed to buy back as confirmed to *Spin* in 2000, 'for a price in the low six figures'.

The break from traditional recording contracts was a big deal at the time. She wasn't making money anyway, so the move to more creative control with less outside influence, was a big step. With the songs now under her control, she co-founded SuperEgo Records with manager Michael Hausman, and finally issued *Bachelor No.2*, which had been largely finished in 1998, herself. This new independent approach has suited Aimee well through the intervening years. At the time, she told *Rolling Stone*, 'I was just so relieved to not have to stay awake at night trying to figure out how to work within a system that's impossible to work with'.

Another bone of contention with Interscope was the cover. They wanted to use Aimee's image, but she was no longer interested in being a cover girl. Gail Marowitz recalled in *Varoom!* in 2009 the 'enormous and exhausting fight' to keep Aimee off the cover: '"Well, she's a pretty girl", and it's like, "Well the record's not about that." If fans want to see what she looks like, go to her website. It became so frustrating'. The finished graphics for *Bachelor No.2* used Victorian engravings to complement the songs. With Gail designing all of her covers since, Aimee puts their productive relationship down to 'One; she has great taste. Two; she has integrity. Three; she will put her money where her mouth is, which to me, after working twenty years for five different record labels, makes the equation so much easier. When you don't have a label complaining about cost, about manufacturing, about where the sticker goes – if there's no place for the sticker, and I'm like "Oh, I should design a cover around a fucking sticker?"'.

With the 'Dodo' subtitle reflecting a feeling that the singer-songwriter was a dying breed, the album was initially sold as a seven-song EP at concerts and via her website, becoming one of the first albums to become successful from online sales, selling 25,000 copies by that route. Riding on a wave of critical acclaim after *Magnolia* (with which this album shares material and is in many ways a counterpart) and the associated Oscar nomination (news of which reached her shortly before a performance in New York, where she told the audience, 'I'm officially declaring myself not an underdog. Maybe an overdog, or like a C-level dog'), Mann's music had its widest audience since early 'Til Tuesday. 'People who saw (*Magnolia*) were kind of forced to give my music a chance', she told *Spin* in 2000, 'so I guess that helped. I can't believe all this is happening because I'm fantastic. Because when it isn't happening, will that be because I'm crappy?'

The Japanese release contained bonus material, while the European version (released on V2 Records) had a slightly different track listing. Reviews were particularly positive, *Spin* reporting that, 'The songs glow and glower in equal parts – full of Carpenters harmonies, vibraphones, and agile vocal leaps that wouldn't sound out of place on a Burt Bacharach album'.

Bachelor No.2 marked the end of her working relationship with Jon Brion. But it was the first release to appear under the auspices of United Musicians, an independent collective formed by Aimee, Michael Penn and Michael Hausman, 'Founded on the principle that every artist should be able to retain copyright ownership of the work they have created, and that this ownership is the basis for artistic strength and true independence'. The UM roster also includes comedians, Aimee holding an affinity for 'their use of language, their specific choice of words and the arrangement of words, as reported in *New York* magazine, in 2017. It's very musical. Jokes might not work if you put certain words at the front of the sentence rather than the back. That's fascinating, and I really admire that'. The link with comedy was extended in 2000, as Mann and Penn formed the *Acoustic Vaudeville* concept – a mixture of music and stand-up comedy – with Janeane Garofalo, Patton Oswalt and David Cross joining them for shows.

US release
'How Am I Different?' (Brion, Mann) (5:03)
Starting with a diffident guitar line and simple programmed drums, piano adds a countermelody in the first verse, gradually coalescing to become strident and confident. The chorus hook is consolidated by a soaring guitar the second time around and through the bridge. The drum programming works well, adding a mechanical texture alongside John Sands' regular kit, Michael Lockwood's guitar letting rip at the end. Overall it's a stylish and forceful opening that immediately grabs the attention.

It could be a breakup song, the protagonist wary of risking it with someone they can no longer trust: 'I can't conceive you're everything you're trying to make me believe'. But it most likely relates to record label issues (they always seem to 'come down on the winner's side'), aware of the unscrupulous workings of the machine and that she's no different to hundreds of others who have been minced by it previously. ''Cause this show is too well designed, Too well to be held with only me in mind'. This interpretation is bolstered by the sardonic bridge: 'And just one question before I pack, When you fuck it up later, Do I get my money back?' – its striking F-Bomb bringing home the song's angst, underlined by its repetition three times towards the close.

'Nothing Is Good Enough' (Mann) (3:10)
Featured as an instrumental in *Magnolia*, here it gets the full lyrical treatment. Plaintive, with a hint of Bacharach in the bitter fairytale-gone-bad opening, the vocals come straight in with piano after a brief Chamberlin figure – both from Benmont Tench – the arrangement remaining simple. Piano stays in steady rhythm against the lush Chamberlin, backing vocals accentuating at key points. But at heart, it's about the vocal melody, telling of another relationship gone sour. 'What was started out with such excitement now I gladly end with relief, In what now has become a familiar motif'. This toxicity could again be the result of label skulduggery. It's a sad song of repeated inevitability, the swinging chorus stating:

That nothing is good enough
For people like you
Who have to have someone take the fall
And something to sabotage
Determined to lose it all

The second verse puts the boot in even harder, observing that 'Critics at their worst could never criticise the way that you do' and 'There's no one else, I find, To undermine or dash a hope, Quite like you', with the exquisite payoff of 'And you do it so casually, too'.

The bridge seems lighthearted at face value, but the words bite again, ending with a cutting 'Wouldn't a smarter man simply walk away?'. After Aimee's voice rises high in the last line of the final chorus, this one-sided relationship ends with a bare restatement of the song's title.

'Red Vines' (Mann) (3:44)

The first single (released in March 2001) moves from a syncopated intro with Michael Penn's guitar, into the first verse where electric piano takes up the vocal support. Guitar harmonics and programmed strings filter in, and the strong chorus opens into a fuller arrangement. With the bridge injecting energy into the final chorus, it's a very nice song and a good single choice, ending on delicate piano.

The Red Vines of the title are a brand of liquorice. In the song, Aimee is the onlooker of a relationship that has nowhere to go, noting that all they really have are cigarettes and the titular sweets. She knows something that would split the pair apart, but is unable to tell, and has to watch from the sidelines.

The second verse features the enigmatic lines, 'So you're running 'round the parking lot, 'til every lightning bug is caught, Punching some pinholes in the lid of a jar, While we wait in the car'. They could refer to the couple's energetic early days, as they now try to keep the excitement alive, not realising that, like captured insects do, the excitement will soon die, as those who look on are aware. There are suggestions that the song is about Paul Thomas Anderson.

Aimee confirmed to *The Performing Songwriter* in 1999 that the opening lines were originally 'They're all still on their honeymoon, It's Underdog Day Afternoon', and that 'For a while there I was actually going to call the record *Underdog Day*'.

'The Fall Of The World's Own Optimist' (Elvis Costello, Mann) (3:06)

There are some golden words here, and plenty of them to fit in, but the pace is stately and there's no rush to do so. Aimee had one verse and a chorus but couldn't finish it, until Elvis Costello 'came along and wrote this whole B-section to the chorus, which was really great. It takes the song in this whole other direction. And then he added in the verse lyrics, which I then had to tailor to get back to the original topic', which seems to involve the idolisation of someone who doesn't deserve it. In that respect, it's likely to be a working relationship, where the singer is cast aside by someone they admire ('The eggshells I've been treading couldn't spare me a beheading ... from a Caesar who was only slumming'), leading to the realisation 'We're only flogging the horse when the horseman has up and died'.

Keyboards add embellishments, the chorus lifting things further, on a swell of backing vocals and spiky guitar. The second verse is stripped back, while the instrumental bridge has a hint of Beatles quirkiness. This is a beautiful song, realised with care.

'Satellite' (Mann) (4:10)

Opening with Patrick Warren's see-sawing piano, Aimee comes in with a
plaintive 'Let's assume you were right', followed by a waltzing brushed snare
and bass drum rhythm. It's a gorgeously warm and dynamic song, the lilting
opening verse calmly suggesting a game that has been played to its conclusion,
with nothing left to do but 'Deflate the stars and put away the sun, And so
we can call it a day'. The chorus pushes the arrangement forward with string
synths and kettle drum flourishes, as Aimee confronts the issue:

> Baby, it's clear, from here
> You're losing your atmosphere
> From here, you're losing it

The reduction back to piano and rhythm includes a mournful brass element
with twinkling percussion, as the enigmatic second verse suggests there is no
defence for the game-playing, and the case 'was lost from the first'. To me, this
all suggests a business rather than personal relationship, and likely refers to the
ephemeral quest for chart success. But it works either way.

The gorgeous bridge rises and falls with keyboard textures, strings and
others, before the final chorus and a guitar-inflected close. The words back up
the artist/label friction, diverging agenda interpretation:

> So have it your way
> Whatever makes the best résumé
> Whatever you can throw in
> Wash, rinse and spin 'til it's spun away
> Okay
> But I won't be sticking around

It's a lovely song, easy to enjoy without digging into the darkness of the lyric.
It's light and airy with a billowing sense of (possibly hard-won) freedom.

'Deathly' (Mann) (5:37)

On *Magnolia* and discussed previously.

'Ghost World' (Mann) (3:30)

A melodic Beatle-esque pop song with melancholy overtones that build from
an arrangement of electric guitars and drums, inspired by Aimee's love of
graphic novels. Daniel Clowes' *Ghost World* was the first one she read, telling
Varoom in 2009: 'I thought it was the greatest thing I had ever seen.'

It's sung from the perspective of *Ghost World* character, Enid. Having
recently graduated from high school, she had planned to go to college but
failed to get in. With 'college out of reach', and fed up with the aimless small-
town existence, she decides to embark on a new life by 'bailing this town'.

However, her most-likely future sees things just continue as they are. There's despair in the seemingly endless waste of simply hanging around. Action is required. As something of a misfit, she feels that 'Everyone I know is acting weird or way too cool', so she spends her time reading or riding her bicycle. There's a growling disquiet to the electric guitar, Aimee convincingly telling Enid's story with the coolness of the outsider.

She seems lost in her situation, and needs 'someone with the brains and the know-how to tell me what I want' – the line delivered with a pleading directness. The perceived pointlessness of her situation ('I'll walk down to the bay and jump off of the dock and watch the summer waste away') seems to stiffen her resolve. But in the final 'So tell me what I want', she still requires confirmation.

I suspect that Aimee empathised with Enid's situation and there's some autobiography to this one. The video, shot in a small-town high school, sees Aimee playing with her band and cycling around the yard, a young girl playing Enid in some scenes. A very enjoyable acoustic version appeared as a 'Calling It Quits' B-side.

'Calling It Quits' (Mann) (4:09)

The second single, released in September 2001. When later asked bt *The Performing Songwriter* how she recovered from faltering inspiration, Aimee cited an interview with Fiona Apple. 'She was talking about making poetry by cutting out headlines from newspapers. So I thought, "That sounds like fun". I wound up with a couple of the lines for 'Calling It Quits' that way. I kept working at it like that and writing stuff down at the same time until it took a shape that meant something to me. Then I just went back and threw out all the other stuff that was just wordplay.'

And there are some great lines here. 'He's a serious Mister, Shake his hand and he'll twist your arm' linking to 'monopoly money' and 'buying the funny farm', suggests a business deal going south. Aimee's doing flips but only being paid in chips. It's a slinky song, right from the floor tom intro as it shuffles on the rhythm, abetted by the electronic vibe from Buddy Judge's programming.

The vocal line lifts seductively into *A Diamond As Big As The Ritz*, taken from the title of F. Scott Fitzgerald's 1922 novella which describes a plantation owner who heads west from Virginia (a parallel with Aimee's starting point) and discovers the world's largest diamond. To keep the secret, he commits heinous acts, including convincing his slaves that the north lost the Civil War, thus keeping them in perpetual bondage. The references to Aimee's experiences under restrictive contracts couldn't be clearer, and bitterness hangs heavy in the air.

The smooth-talking lies continue, the 'ruby slippers' just a fantasy to cover up for the booby-trapped path – 'There's no prize, just a smaller size'. She's stuck.

Now he's numbering himself among the masterminds
'Cause he's hit upon the leverage of valentines
Lifting dialogue from Judy Garland storylines

It's keyboard-heavy, but in a textural way, adding Chamberlin, piano and Wurlitzer for a dream-like backing. The vocal is upfront with a delicious echo, lifting off with edgy guitar from Lockwood. The backing vocals are dreamy too, with subtle string sounds and trumpet additions filling out a tantalising whole. It's a beautifully mature song that ebbs to voice and acoustic guitar alone, 'Where get-tough girls turn into goldmines', before Lockwood solos.

'But oh, Those Polaroid babies, Taking chances with rabies, Happy to tear me to bits'. Ultimately, all she can do is quit. This ticks all the boxes, taking its time and building to an all-hands-on-deck finish before the fade. It's one of this fine album's many highlights.

'Driving Sideways' (Michael Lockwood, Mann) (3:49)
On *Magnolia* and discussed previously. It wasn't included on the album's European version.

'Just Like Anyone' (Mann) (1:22)
Aimee has said that she wrote this when Jeff Buckley died in 1997.

I hadn't known Jeff extremely well, but we kept bumping into each other here and there. One night we met for a drink at a pub in NYC and started writing messages to each other on a paper placemat that was there, instead of talking, because the music in the bar was really loud or something. An interesting effect of that was that we found ourselves writing things that we would never dare to say to each other out loud. I remember thinking that he seemed to be sort of lost and sad, although he outwardly was very funny and lively and confident, and wrote something about that, among other things. I didn't talk to him for a long time after that. I went to England to live for a while and we talked once or twice and then nothing for over a year. Then one night I got a voicemail message from him that said, 'I just realised what you were trying to tell me that night'. I tried to call him back, but the number I had for him was old, and then I got his new number but I was out of town again and it was difficult to call, and then I heard that he was missing, and presumed dead.

The lyric is sad, burdened with loss, the first verse saying it all:

So maybe I wasn't that good a friend
But you were one of us
And I will wonder
Just like anyone
If there was something else I could've done

The second verse follows it up with 'Your cry for help was oh so very faint, But still I heard and knew something was wrong, Just nothing you could put your finger on'.

At a little under a minute-and-a-half, it's an intense burst of regret for not having been able to help a friend in dark times. Quietly contemplative, a slow and sweet lament, the acoustic guitar and fragile voice are joined by Chamberlin and celeste, to give an antique orchestration.

'Susan' (Mann) (3:51)

Electric guitar with a programmed rhythm makes for an upbeat start, moving into acoustic guitar with keyboards. Aimee's voice is double-tracked in the chorus, the exemplary embellishments from Michael Lockwood adding gritty melody, including a brief and woozy solo. The third verse pulls things back, with Michael Penn's lovely backing, and the song trails off with 20 seconds of chiming guitar.

The lyric describes the realisation that a friend's warnings have proven correct: 'A prognosis that was hopeless, From the very first domino'. The cheeriness of the melody throws you sideways when you realise that the song is a hindsight acknowledgement, of the singer's mistakes – initially hidden amongst 'The flash of the fuse, The smell of cordite' – and of being too close to the problem to fully realise the implications. Sometimes you need someone looking at things from a distance to see the full picture. But things are spun around in the chorus with 'And someday he will live to regret me, Susan, I can see it now'. Has Susan been warning that the singer's actions are the problem, the damage done causing her to end the relationship for his sake? He had 'thrown her a rope', but 'We kissed for a while to see how it played, and pulled the pin on another grenade'. There may have been hope that things would be resolved, and regret when that wasn't possible ('It may be pure illusion, But it's beautiful while it's here'), but the deed had to be done. After the event, she acknowledges that it wasn't easy ('I had some trouble with the goodbye'), having finally set off the fireworks to end things with a bang: 'I checked my roman candle supply, And watched the vapor trail in the sky'.

'It Takes All Kinds' (Brion, Mann) (4:06)

As we were speaking of the devil
You walked right in
Wearing hubris like a medal
You revel in
But it's me at whom you'll level
Your javelin

The scene is set with the now excessive pride and self-confidence of a former friend. The singer can no longer stand it and is surprised at herself for even thinking he could change. He is perceived as 'Throwing (his) weight around the sun', with a rueful realisation that he's 'Happier now that you've become what you hated'.

From the easy rhythmic intro, there's an airy 1960s feel with sighing backing vocals. Initially, she had wanted him and is disappointed with herself: 'I'm surprised I even thought I had half a chance, I was just one in a million of also-rans'. She reminisces about the early days of their friendship, the reference to Burt Bacharach fitting in perfectly with the feel of the song. Times were happy, 'You loved the world you lived in and it loved you back', but 'Now you look out for number one ... I guess it takes all kinds'.

Built on piano with strummed acoustic guitar, the arrangement is simple. But the space within it and the lightness achieved, delivers the song to perfection – the pointed words swathed in a beautiful melody. Again, Michael Lockwood's stabs of electric guitar add greatly.

'You Do' (Mann) (3:43)
On *Magnolia* and discussed previously.

Related Tracks
'Save Me' (Mann) (4:35) (Japan bonus track and European version)
Discussed in the *Magnolia* section, the single reached 88 in the UK. The video was also included on the Japanese version (which was the same as the US, with the addition of the song and video) and European release (which featured a different track ordering with one swapped completely).

'Backfire' (Brion, Mann) (3:25) (European version)
Added to the European release in place of 'Driving Sideways', it's a breakdown of communication in a seemingly dysfunctional relationship. With cookies, junk food and beers in hand, it's time for some fun, but already she's 'all out of any explanation of what I'm on about', as his decision-making gets them into difficult situations. There's nothing she can do to stop it happening. She knows that things will go wrong for them, but he pushes ahead anyway, causing frustration. 'Your intentions were grand, But it's out of my hands, And it isn't the way I pictured it either'. She doesn't believe what he says anymore, cringing when they end up in yet another tricky spot. He says it's not a problem and to sit tight. 'There's always a hitch, That will cause the whole thing to backfire'. She knows he wants to be the one to get them out of trouble and save the day, like a St. Bernard in an avalanche, leading to the delightful lines, 'But in my panic, I may pull too hard, And the novice lifeguard, Gets rushed off in the ambulance', as the planned rescue fails.

It's poppy and upbeat, in the same vein as *I'm With Stupid*. Fun and happy, but it's all going haywire within. Buddy Judge's backing vocals are punchy; the keyboard, percussion and guitar additions all well-placed; and the ending hints at *Sgt. Pepper* zaniness.

Lost in Space (2002)

Personnel:
Aimee Mann: Vocals, Bass Guitar, Upright Bass, Acoustic, Electric and 12-string
Guitars, Piano, Keyboards, Drums & Percussion, Sound Effects
Jay Bellerose, John Sands: Drums
Jebin Bruni: Chamberlin, Piano, Prophet 5, Synthesiser Strings
Denyse Buffum, Carole Mukogawa: Violas
Darius Campo, Susan Chatman, Joel Derouin, Armen Garabedian, Berj Garabedian,
Peter Kent, Natalie Leggett, Mario de León, Michele Richards, John Wittenberg:
Violins
Larry Corbett, Steve Richards, Dan Smith: Cellos
Mike Denneen: Harpsichord, Electric Piano, Wurlitzer
Jason Falkner: Bass Guitar
Ryan Freeland: Clappers, Drum Loops, Radio Sound Effects
Buddy Judge, Mike Randle, Rusty Squeezebox, Darian Sahanaja: Background Vocals
Suzie Katayama: Conductor
Michael Lockwood: Acoustic, Electric, Baritone, Slide, 12-string and bass guitars,
Autoharp, Celeste, Chamberlin, Dobro, E-bow, Harmonium, Keyboards, Synthesisers,
Leslie Pedal, Drum Loops, Marxophone, Percussion, Sound Effects, Theremin, Zither
Seth McClain: Clappers
Joe Meyer: French Horn
Dave Palmer: Organ
Michael Penn: Drum Loops
Jonathan Quarmby: Horn & String Arrangements
David Stone: Upright Bass
Patrick Warren: Chamberlin, Marxophone, Synthesiser Strings
Producers: Mike Denneen, Ryan Freeland, Michael Lockwood
Record Label: SuperEgo, V2
Recorded: Stampede Origin Studios, Sonora Recorders, Henson Recording Studios,
Q Division, Kampo
Released: 27 August 2002
Running Time: 43:03
Highest chart place: US:35, UK:72

Lost in Space was assembled over eighteen months and released in August
2002, a *Special Edition* double-disc version following in 2003. It stands alone
in Aimee's catalogue, featuring a more heavily-produced and experimental
sound, which I thoroughly enjoy. For me, it is one of her finest works. From
Billboard in 2002:

> We'd get a few songs together, then we'd go out and do some shows, and then
> we'd return to the studio and work on some more new songs. It made for a nice
> creative rhythm. There was no need to rush around and worry about not having
> enough songs for the album by the time we wanted to release something.

The theme of addiction shines through, unsurprising as Aimee confirmed that she'd been reading a lot about drug and alcohol dependency over the last few years. The songs are, as always, insightful, pointed where necessary, and beautifully arranged.

Critical approval was overwhelming, the lyrics and melodies noted amid this new textured and complex sound. *Mojo* praised Michael Lockwood's production, while *Billboard* called it 'sonically rich', containing some of Mann's 'most intimate storytelling'. However, *Rolling Stone* was less positive, complaining that the songs lacked changes in pace. Sales remained modest, despite the acclaim.

The cover artwork, accompanying mini-comic and full-page illustrations (including a cartoon image of Aimee), were created by Canadian graphic novelist, Gregory Gallant (artist of the long-running *Palookaville* series), under his pen name Seth. As she said to *Varoom* in 2009, Aimee considered him for *Lost in Space*, 'because there's such a tone of melancholy that goes through his work, plus he uses that very old-school fifties single-panel style'. The resulting near-monochrome drawings reflect the tone of the music – sci-fi sound effects leading into songs of failure, paranoia and hope. Although he remembered 'Til Tuesday, Seth was not familiar with Aimee's solo work. But he quickly got what she was trying to do: 'It was a beautiful album – deep, emotional, profound'. He enjoyed the freedom of the working process, 'stopped thinking of the job as just a commercial project, and actually took it to heart as a piece of my real work'. Aimee regarded the results as 'a weird sort of imagery subtext that's in the music and also in the lyrics, and it was perfect'.

Shortly after the release of *Lost in Space*, Aimee and her band played James Taylor's 'Shed A Little Light' on *The West Wing*, and appeared in *Buffy the Vampire Slayer* performing 'This Is How It Goes' and 'Pavlov's Bell', the latter appearing on the *Buffy* soundtrack album, *Radio Sunnydale – Music from the TV Series*. Aimee also had a line of dialogue: 'Man, I hate playing vampire towns.'

'Humpty Dumpty' (Mann) (4:01)

Released as a single in October 2002, the analogy of Humpty's terminal fall is recreated in the first verse, the singer no longer feeling who she was. Although it sounds like a conversation, much of the song can be regarded as someone talking to themselves about a breakdown that has thrown a relationship sideways to the point where the couple can't relate to what they used to believe. She wants to feel the way she did, imagining herself split into fragments, 'And none of the pieces would talk to you'. The chorus suggests escape: 'Better take the keys and drive forever, Staying won't put these futures back together'. But it's not clear who should leave, as 'All the perfect drugs and superheroes, Wouldn't be enough to bring me up to zero', and there is no real solution for either of them.

Something has happened to cause this situation. They probably both changed, but the sense of fear and depression is palpable. It seems she might be going through some mental issues, possibly drug-related, and can't see a way back. The partner is supportive and has more belief in the future they could have together, not believing that the situation is the final nail. 'But I'm not the girl you once put your faith in, just someone who looks like me'. She urges him to get out while he can: 'I'm pouring quicksand and sinking is all I have planned, So better just go', the final words bringing the Humpty Dumpty analogy to a conclusion:

All the king's horses and all the king's men
Couldn't put baby together again

Michael Lockwood's lugubrious guitar sets the scene over a steady rhythm, adding twinkling phrases in the background before stepping up in full support of the chorus. It's a lush arrangement of Chamberlin and piano that sets the scene for one of Aimee's most expansive albums. The song itself has a pretty basic structure. But that, and the hook, help to deliver the intensity of the words.

'High On Sunday 51' (Paul Dalen, Mann) (3:15)
Written with road manager, Paul Dalen, on which subject she spoke to *Rolling Stone*:

He was starting to write songs and write lyrics, and he was asking my advice. He played me the music he had written to them, which was kind of a little too happy, and I said, 'In my opinion, because these lyrics are so dark, you have to have music that kind of mirrors that darkness, because otherwise it doesn't make sense. When you have a line that's like, "Let me be your heroin", you have to really back it up with something that's a little more serious, otherwise it sounds like you're just kidding around'. So I wrote some music as an example, and then as I was working on it, I was like, 'You know, I really like this'.

The title is enigmatic, but the lyric is pretty clear about drug use being involved – specifically heroin, the craving used as a simile for unrequited love, 'Creating want by holding back' like 'some reverse pyromaniac'. The pleading 'Let me try' is a sinister payoff, as the *drug* calls, the music dark yet yearning. *Rock's Back Pages* described it as 'Blurry, with smeary slide guitar between cut-glass vocals, stained mood, dark-toned and grainy'.

It's sultry to start, turning to pleading as things get desperate in the waltz-time chorus, Aimee's vocal beautifully supported by Buddy Judge. 'I turn my back to lure you in' – but it's not working, he needs her to 'Let me be your heroin'. The self-loathing in 'Hate the sinner but love the sin' suggests that the liaison may be forbidden – adultery perhaps? This is borne out in the third verse, where a fateful course of action is committed to (alluding to Julius Caesar crossing the Rubicon river, thus precipitating a war). There is no going back. The ship of his desire runs aground with sweeping Chamberlin strings.

'The ship awash our rudder gone, The rats have fled but I'm hanging on'. But he's still pleading with her to 'Let me try'.

'Lost in Space' (Mann) (3:28)

Mike Denneen's Wurlitzer piano suggests the title's space analogy, played out in the first verse description of 'A bubble drifting into a place where planets shift and the moon's erased, It's features lift in the glare', suggesting an easy-going free spirit. However, the second verse confirms that interactions with others are 'mostly bluff' and about 'just pretending to care', lost in a vacuum, 'Gone but I don't know where'. It seems to be describing an emotional disconnect with a partner – the one who 'pretends to care', but offers nothing of substance, simply filling empty space.

There's sarcasm in the suggestion that she fronts the relationship while he just falls into place behind her ('She's the face and I'm the double'), unable to 'Tell the line from the parallel'. Aimee is here accompanied by exquisite backing vocals in the bridge, followed by a soaring double-tracked solo from Lockwood. The song ends with a warning to others to 'beware'. It could be an internal vision of anxiety and depression, concerned about the detachment she feels from others, faking happiness while outsiders describe her as she used to be.

Lockwood's guitar is everywhere, thrusting with unusual tones and unorthodox choices, lifting the song to a new level. Chamberlin colours the spaces amid textural instrumentation, supporting the confident vocal, a fading chord ending in distant birdsong. It's loosely melodic, without the need for any definite hooks.

'This Is How It Goes' (Mann) (3:47)

The delicate acoustic opening is beautifully melodic, Aimee's voice particularly fragile as she seems to be dealing with a partner with anger issues, probably resulting from the drug habit and associated shame mentioned as the song builds into a full and hooky chorus. The clanging of bells in the first verse brings in the *Round One* boxing analogy as she can't stop what's going to happen next. As a result, she 'won't go near the market place, With what I'm selling lately, 'Cause this is how it goes', keeping her true feelings hidden to avoid conflict. The sinister edge of the third verse suggests the anger turning physical:

One more failure to connect
With so many how could I object?
And you, what on earth did you expect?
Well, I can't tell you, baby
When this is how it goes

But she's going to 'try to hold on' while he looks to kick the habit on his own terms. They won't talk about it and whether he has been successful, 'But baby I'll know, Baby I'll know'.

This is a beautiful and haunting song, coloured by Chamberlin brass and strings, and the ubiquitous electric guitar textures. A live version was included in the album's *Special Edition*.

'Guys Like Me' (Mann) (3:12)

Bare chords from Lockwood set up this wry and cynical look at guys for whom outward appearance is everything, macho posturing covering for a lack of emotional substance. It's about the games they play to convince prospective partners that they're the real deal and worth investing time in, but they lack the empathy to make relationships work. 'We pull you close but never really, Looking warm but feeling chilly'. They don't have to try too hard. Their physical side attracts all the women they want, so why put in the hard yards? Guys like these 'block the circulation 'til we're all completely numb', there is no 'payoff in the final reel', and they're generally not the people to rely on for a 'forever' partnership.

The pace is slow; the first two verses incorporating more detail as the sound expands. The bridge adds a change of tone before Lockwood's wonderful soloing, flowing and building into a double-tracked finale. The boxing analogy comes through again in 'Put your money on a bona-fide heavyweight' (rather than these superficial charlatans).

'Pavlov's Bell' (Mann) (4:27)

Fuelled by Chamberlin from the spacey opening and throughout, there's a 1950s sci-fi feel, the chorus properly kicking things out with Lockwood's guitar shards. The pace is steady, but this is most definitely a rock song.

On a long bus trip, the singer urges Mario to come clean and 'Tell me what I already know'. But inside she knows 'that we can't talk about it' because he won't communicate how he feels. The chorus suggests that she keeps trying to talk, 'ringing Pavlov's bell' and, like the salivating hounds, getting the same response every time. She's in denial, trying to tell herself that they can discuss things, but knowing inside, that it's a false hope.

Lockwood's solo around the forceful melody line before the third verse has a deranged edge that perfectly captures the frustration, restated at the close. Aimee's voice in that verse is more demanding – he's still telling her there's nothing wrong, but she knows he's lying, finding it impossible to suppress her doubts:

If you're what I need
Then only you can save me
So come on baby, give me the fix
And let's just talk about it

It ends with a plaintive repeat of that last line before a climactic 'So baby, show and tell!'

In the video we see Aimee waking, then wandering around the house in a red velvet jacket, ending up back in bed where she began.

'Real Bad News' (Mann) (3:53)

There's a spacey air of Chamberlin, theremin and organ, with the vocal melody set above, before drums and guitars prowl in. Aimee has decided he's not worth bothering with – he's the 'real bad news'. It appears that he 'can get some things confused, Like whose secrets are whose', suggesting that the issue has sprung from information that wasn't his to impart. She chastises him for suggesting that he knows how she feels and that things will change: 'you don't' and 'they won't'. Reality is intruding into the lovely pictures that he has painted, and she can no longer 'stem the tide of overwhelm'. She doesn't hold back, pointing out that he tries 'to keep it going, But a lot of avenues just aren't open to you when you're real bad news'. The next verse lays everything out quite plainly as Aimee sings 'I've got love and anger, They come as a pair' – a brooding sense of the latter apparent in the sparse arrangement, bursts of guitar suggesting that the rage will soon be unleashed.

> You can take your chances
> But buyer beware
> And I won't make you feel bad
> When I show you
> This big ball of sad isn't
> Worth even filling with air

Unusually for Mann there's a 'la la la' sung part before the final verse, giving a light touch to a song of rebellion against injustice. The *Special Edition* included a live version.

'Invisible Ink' (Mann, Clayton Scoble) (4:59)

One of only a couple of co-writes on *Lost in Space*, the music written with Clayton Scoble, a collaborator since latter-day 'Til Tuesday, although he doesn't play on this album.

It starts calmly, just acoustic guitar and voice, and the almost matter-of-fact opening lines, 'There comes a time when you swim or sink, So I jumped in the drink, 'Cause I couldn't make myself clear'. It's another song of communication breakdown, in a sparse and low-key arrangement.

> Maybe I wrote in invisible ink
> Oh I've tried to think
> How I could have made it appear

The message just won't get through. 'I feel like a ghost who's trying to move your hands, Over some ouija board in the hopes I can spell out my name' feels like a cry for attention. The 'magic at first glance is just sleight of hand, Depending on what you believe', but ultimately 'Something gets lost when you translate ... Perspective is everything'.

There's sadness in 'I suppose I should be happy to be misread, Better be that than some of the other things I have become'. But she tries to add pathos and laugh it off: 'The plot is cliched, The jokes are stale, And baby we've all heard it all before' – nobody needs 'details of a love I can't sell anymore'.

This is a deeply personal song, delivered openly and honestly. Is it a breakup song? Probably, and possibly as a result of addiction, as per the core theme. But whatever the detail, the delivery is heartfelt. It might be a failed attempt to tell someone that you love them. As always, communication is key in any relationship, and she's pointing out that it isn't always as simple as that.

The longest song on the album, it picks the words carefully, to try and explain the feelings at hand with bare voice and guitar, strings swelling gently to add warmth. It's all about the voice. Not until the final verse do drums and guitars come in to lift the pace, but it ends where it began. Again, the *Special Edition* includes a live version.

'Today's The Day' (Mann) (4:42)

To save a relationship, you sometimes need to change a situation that you find yourself in, to actively do something about it or 'pack your bags and run':

> Or maybe you can sit and hope
> That providence will fray the rope
> And sink like a stone

The second verse is accusing in tone ('And isn't that enough for you?'), but he's contemplating leaving, to 'send it to oblivion', Aimee singing in her highest register. It looks like he'll metaphorically escape to live anonymously, away from the problem, and 'do what you do, 'til it buries you'.

The final verse is interesting, referencing 'Major Reno at the bluff, Wondering aloud if help is on the way' – the decisions Marcus Reno made at the Battle of the Little Bighorn in 1876, most likely costing General Custer and his men their lives. Here, this is his chance to 'make a break with circumstance, And isn't it enough to prove today's the day?'.

From the spacey intro, the pace is slow, with twinkling embellishments. The brief chorus draws in electric guitar with a splash of sound, the voice supported by backing singers and keyboard brass, making the sparser verses all the more powerful. Lockwood again shines with a solo at the end, before the crackling antique outro.

'The Moth' (Mann) (3:46)

The attraction to the flame of dangerous hook-ups is an addiction that some cannot turn down. They know they might get burned, but it's all part of the excitement, 'And once he's in, He can't go back, He'll beat his wings 'til he burns them black'.

And nothing fuels a good flirtation
Like need and anger and desperation

The chorus raises the stakes. 'So come on let's go, Ready or not, 'Cause there's a flame I know hotter than hot, And with a fuse that's so thoroughly shot away'. The final verse describes the flames of passion burning low. But for those sucked in, the belief persists that there might be an afterglow where it lingers – 'All you really need is the love of heat'.

The tempo is raised for this song, performed entirely by Aimee and Michael Lockwood. Chamberlin phrases suggest the likely doomed flight of the moth. Acoustic guitar drives the verses, the chorus increasing the propulsive feel, after which there's a delicious solo supported by string effects. The *Special Edition* includes a live version.

'It's Not' (Mann) (3:27)

The singer is stuck in a rut, 'going 'round and 'round on the same old circuit ... From behind the screen it can look so perfect, But it's not.' She's at a stoplight in life, waiting to make a change, but she doesn't know what it should be or how to achieve it:

So red turns into green, turning into yellow
But I'm just frozen here on the same old spot
And all I have to do is press the pedal
But I'm not
No, I'm not

She has a dilemma, something secret that she needs to be careful about sharing, because as soon as she does, 'kiss it goodbye'. That thought stops her from moving forward. It's easier to pretend that things are fine instead of taking risks, and there's a deep feeling of loneliness and, ultimately, uselessness.

The final verse brings things full-circle. She decides to stay where she is, in the past where she knows how things work, with the one she thinks can resolve the situation, but that isn't the case.

So baby kiss me like a drug, like a respirator
And let me fall into the dream of the astronaut
Where I get lost in space that goes on forever
And you make all the rest just an afterthought
And I believe it's you who could make it better
But it's not
No, it's not

The relationship is addictive but ultimately futile, with a sad realisation in the bitterness of the final words. It's a melancholic way to end an album of deep darkness and loss, but it's beautiful. The voice and acoustic guitar are gradually joined by strings, bass and eventually, a basic drum rhythm, in a sensitive and rewarding arrangement. The song was previously introduced in concert as 'The most depressing song I've ever written'. It has a lot of competition! The *Special Edition* includes a live version.

Related Tracks
The Lost in Space: Special Edition includes the following tracks on its bonus disc.

'The Scientist' (Live) (Guy Berryman, Jonny Buckland, Will Champion, Chris Martin) (4:19)
Originally from Coldplay's 2002 album *A Rush of Blood to the Head*. Aimee's voice is warm and enticing. Supported by piano, she does such a fantastic job, it could have been written for her. The arrangement expands as it progresses, becoming an epic before falling back to simplicity to close.

'Nightmare Girl' (Mann) (3:49)
This B-side of 'Humpty Dumpty' is a dark tale of a girl spiralling toward self-destruction. Probably demoted from the album as the upbeat nature would have been too jarring, the easy pace with strings and a strong, expansive chorus, is classic Mann:

> Things are getting weirder
> At the speed of light
> Nightmare girl
> All this fever dreaming kills my appetite
> For another restless night

It's sung from the male perspective, continually confused by the excesses that *nightmare girl* craves, her addictive personality leading her towards danger. The bridge describes an attempted late-night rescue, and the wishful thought that he can save her from herself – 'I gotta go and make it OK'. But it seems inevitable that things will continue to get weirder.

'Fighting The Stall' (Mann) (4:04)
From a shuffling opening riff, drums and guitars crash in with muscle. The melodic verses soar, ending with a minimal chorus of the title line repeated twice. The title may be opaque, but the opening verse makes it clear, with flying analogising a relationship:

> And if we survive takeoff
> The chances of accidents are small
> As long as there's some procedure
> For fighting the stall

The second verse takes in 'drawing straws to see just who will get the duty free', an autopilot situation of 'running on fumes and alcohol', waiting for a potential moment of truth where the stall might occur. Keyboard textures feature after the bridge, when things start to slide:

> And I'll go down in flames just for the hell of it all
> Because I couldn't take
> Standing in place
> Waiting to fall

There's a doomed attempted landing as they 'spiral into a fireball', harmony vocals colouring the outro. And it was all going so well! Another great lost song.

'Observatory' (4:19) (Mann, Glenn Tilbrook)

Written with Glenn Tilbrook, it's a winner, kicking off immediately with jangly guitars into a chugging verse. It's an affair between a single man and a married woman. They 'started the clock' and 'watched the sweeping second hand', waiting for the almost inevitable, which comes in the second verse, sung by Tilbrook:

> Fun is fun, but when push comes to shove
> When it's done, we'll deny it was love
> She will say 'Jim, this was a mistake'

The scene returns to the observatory described in the driving and tuneful chorus, bookended by the lines 'But at least I was calm'. Aimee and Glenn duet in the bridge, summing up the outcome:

> And you'll be glad to leave with dignity intact
> She won't be sad so much as matter-of-fact
> Like it was doomed and hopeless as a suicide pact

It's evocative, and conjures some lovely images. An excellent upbeat song.

Live at St. Ann's Warehouse (2004)

Personnel:
Aimee Mann: Vocals, Acoustic and Electric Guitar, Bass, Piano
Julian Coryell: Guitars, Melodica, Backing Vocals
Jebin Bruni: Keyboards
Paul Bryan: Bass Guitar, Acoustic Guitar, Backing Vocals
John Sands: Drums
Producers: Barry Ehrmann, Pierre Lamoureux
Record Label: SuperEgo
Recorded: St. Ann's Warehouse, Brooklyn, New York, 22-24 June 2004
Released: 2 November 2004
Running Time: 58:20 CD, 80:00 approx. DVD
Highest chart place: US: -, UK: -

Recorded over three nights at New York's St. Ann's Warehouse in June 2004, Aimee's only official live album was released as a two-disc package, thirteen-track CD and sixteen-track DVD, with live footage directed by Pierre Lamoureux. The set covers all Aimee's solo albums to date, with the bias resting on the latest three, with four songs each. *Whatever* appears twice with 'Wise Up' from *Magnolia*. There are also premiers for two songs from the forthcoming *The Forgotten Arm* (Aimee suggesting that it was due to be called *King of the Jailhouse*). The set is packed with many of her sharpest songs, but the booklet shows the set-list from the second show of the run, containing an additional four songs. It's a shame these didn't find a place on the DVD, but as it is, it's a punchy record of Aimee's live shows of the time.

Mann largely sticks with acoustic guitar, with Paul Bryan on bass and acoustic guitar (a band member since 1999), Julian Coryell on guitars and melodica (two years in the band), Jebin Bruni on keyboards (four years), and John Sands (who first played with Aimee in 1993 and recorded with her since *I'm With Stupid*) on drums. Bryan and Coryell supply backing vocals. This release marked the start of Aimee's continuing recording relationship with Paul Bryan.

It's a good representation of the concert experience, with close-ups, sweeping pans and wide shots. It's a warm environment, the curtain backdrop effectively delivering lighting and projections behind the sparse stage – Coryell stage-left, Bruni stage-right, and Aimee at the front in white jacket and jeans with a wide blue tie. The tight band performs arrangements that differ minimally from the originals, Aimee often singing with eyes tightly shut, getting fully into the mood. Her interactions with the audience are engaging and friendly, and she injects a lot of fun, her exquisite comic timing coming across as endearingly unrehearsed and genuine. She explains her recent interest in boxing, wryly describing herself as a 'not very robust physical specimen', and musing on the possibility of organising a tour with other boxing songwriters and having bouts between sets: 'Dylan is 20 years older than me, I could probably take him'.

Regarding humour at shows, she told *Chicago Music Guide* in 2007:

There's probably a little bit of relief of 'Oh, I'm so glad that she's not super-sour and depressed' – so any small joke, I get the laughter of relief, if it's funny at all! Half the shows I still go, 'Oh, I don't know what to say', but I've definitely learned a lot from just being around comics. That's not to say that I'm funny, but I think just being around it and adopting a little bit of a cadence or vernacular, is helpful.

'The Moth' settles the band in, 'Calling It Quits' featuring melodica and synthesisers to cover the accordion and trumpet parts. A rocking 'Sugarcoated' is prefaced by a cheerful 'Buenas Noches!' from Aimee, Coryell delivering the Bernard Butler parts splendidly, before 'Going Through the Motions', a fine taster for *The Forgotten Arm*.

Coryell adds slide to 'Humpty Dumpty', Aimee switching to bass for 'Amateur', with lovely piano from Bruni. Sands' brushed snare gives an intimate feel alongside dusky soloing. 'Wise Up' keeps the relaxed mood in a heartfelt version as she moves back to acoustic (Coryell noting in the interview section that 'every time she plays that song, it hurts me in the most wonderful way'). Sticking with *Magnolia*, a poignant 'Save Me' raises the tempo, with melodica and electrifying guitar, Sands playing drum rhythms with his left hand, percussion with his right.

'Stupid Thing' bolsters the energy levels, followed by (on CD only) a swinging 'That's Just What You Are'. A rocking take on 'Pavlov's Bell' includes another excellent Coryell solo, Mann moving to electric rhythm for 'Long Shot', a great way to end the main set.

The encore begins with a fragile version of '4th Of July', acoustic guitar supported by Bruni's keyboards and Bryan's backing vocals, fully retaining the charm of the original. 'Red Vines' features Mann's acoustic, the rest of the band returning for the chorus, but in a stripped-back version, drums added from the bridge, for a full band finale.

Before 'Invisible Ink', Mann confides that she hates audience participation, but 'I entreat you with all that I have, to join us in this endeavour'. During the practice run-through, she humorously notes that 'There's four fucking people clapping!', but they soon catch on. The performance itself starts bare and acoustic with just Aimee's guitar and voice, before reintroducing the band.

New song, 'King Of The Jailhouse', is introduced as being 'about bitterness, unhappiness and dysfunction. Oh, wait a minute, that's all my songs!'. Mann plays piano here, with slide from Coryell. Finally, 'Deathly' enthrals the crowd with Coryell's powerhouse take on Michael Lockwood's awesome guitar parts.

The DVD includes behind-the-scenes tour footage (with a piano and voice version of 'Way Back When' as soundtrack), plus a slideshow of the St. Ann's shows (played to 'Guys Like Me'). For the interviews, the band and their boss are spoken to separately. Aimee notes that touring is easier now she has more control, but she prefers short periods away travelling with close and trusted friends. Her bandmates suggest she likes it more than she thinks, although Sands says she merely tolerates it. She acknowledges that she still finds applause and audience adoration awkward, and semi-jokingly notes that the songs she prefers are those that are easiest to sing. Overall, it might not be the most exciting concert film you'll ever see, but it's a fine record of Aimee's performances.

The Forgotten Arm (2005)

Personnel:
Aimee Mann: Vocals, Acoustic and Electric Guitars
Jay Bellerose, Victor Indrizzo: Drums and Percussion
Jeff Trott: Electric and Baritone Guitars, Mandolin
Paul Bryan: Bass, Background Vocals
Jebin Bruni: Keyboards
Julian Coryell: Electric Guitar, Slide Guitar, Backing Vocals, Keyboards
The West End Horns: Mark Fisher (Tenor Saxophone), Jason Thor (Trombone),
Willie Murillo (Trumpet, Arrangements)
Chris Bruce: Electric Guitar
Producer: Joe Henry
Record Label: SuperEgo
Recorded: Sunset Sound, The Sound Factory
Released: 3 May 2005
Running Time: 47:06
Highest chart place: US:60, UK:84

Produced by singer-songwriter Joe Henry, and recorded mostly live with few overdubs, *The Forgotten Arm* is striking as Aimee's first concept album. Like *Lost in Space*, it's a study of addiction, telling the story of John (a Vietnam veteran and boxer) and Caroline (a photographer) from their meeting in the 1970s at the Virginia State Fair, where he is fighting exhibition rounds. They run away together to escape their problems, but John's alcoholism only makes matters worse. Written 'as a sort of soundtrack to an imaginary movie', the album is dedicated 'For the alcoholic and addict who still suffers'.

As she confirmed to *Interview* in 2009, Aimee had become interested in boxing, predominantly to keep 'really interested as a way to exercise. It's very strenuous, but because you're so mentally occupied, you don't realise how strenuous it is until the bell rings and you're like "I think I'm going to throw up"'. With this as a growing focus, 'The whole boxing-as-metaphor was looming large in my imagination', the album becoming a reflection of this. The title derives from a boxing move, where one arm is used to hit the opponent, causing him to *forget* about the other, which then delivers the harsher blow. 'The knockout punch is always the one you never see coming.' Discussing her boxing abilities with *Rock 'n' Reel*, she said, 'I'm good enough to know how impossible it is to be really good. Right now, my goal is to throw a good right hand. I do a little bit of sparring. I don't punch hard, I'm slow, my reflexes are slow, I can't really take a punch, I bruise really easily. I got it all!'.

At an exhibition in Los Angeles, she discovered Owen Smith's boxing paintings. The first image she saw was a boxer slumped on his stool. 'It's got this feeling of despair, and when I first saw that, I was like, "That should be the cover".' as she told *Varoom!* in 2009. To format the album like a book,

Right: Aimee Mann through the ages. From the video for 'Til Tuesday's first single, 'Voices Carry', from 1985 directed by DJ Webster.

Left: Aimee in June 2004 at a run of shows at St. Ann's Warehouse in Brooklyn, which later appeared as her only official live release so far.

Below: Aimee in 2017 during an interview to discuss the release of her latest album, *Mental Illness*.

Above: Aimee poses with herself in a still from the video for 1985's 'Love in a Vacuum', the third single from the *Voices Carry* album.

Right: 'Til Tuesday's debut album, *Voices Carry*. A Top twenty hit and their biggest seller, containing the band's most successful pop hits. (*Epic Records*)

Right: *Welcome Home*, 'Til Tuesday's second album from 1986, developed the band's sound but proved less popular than its predecessor. (*Epic Records*)

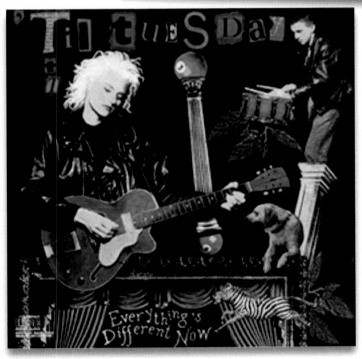

Left: *Everything's Different Now*, 1988. The third and final 'Til Tuesday album moved from new wave pop towards a more singer/songwriter character. (*Epic Records*)

Left: 'Til Tuesday on *American Bandstand* in 1985. Aimee Mann, Michael Hausman and Joey Pesce are interviewed by Dick Clark. (*ABC Television*)

Right: Aimee in the video for 'What About Love', the first single from 1986's *Welcome Home*. Directed by Richard Levine and Ken Ross.

Left: 'Til Tuesday play 'Coming Up Close' live in 1986 (l to r: Joey Pesce, Aimee Mann, Michael Hausman, Robert Holmes).

Right: Robert Holmes and Joey Pesce in the 'Looking Over My Shoulder' video from 1985. Directed by Mick Haggerty.

Left: 'Til Tuesday on *Letterman*, 1 December 1988. They played 'Rip In Heaven', followed by an interview with Michael and Aimee.

Right: 1988's '(Believed You Were) Lucky' video, from Everything's Different Now. Aimee is accompanied by herself, Michael Hausman and Jon Brion.

Left: *Whatever*, Aimee's debut solo album, released on Imago Records in May 1993. The first of many collaborations with art director Gail Marowitz. (*Imago*)

Right: Aimee's second solo album was delayed due to label issues, but *I'm With Stupid* finally appeared on Geffen Records in November 1995. (*Geffen*)

Right: The soundtrack to Paul Thomas Anderson's 1999 film *Magnolia*, released on Warner Music, opened up Aimee's songs to a wider audience. (*Warner*)

Left: After Aimee became disillusioned with major labels, *Bachelor No.2* was the first release on Aimee's SuperEgo label in 2000. (*SuperEgo*)

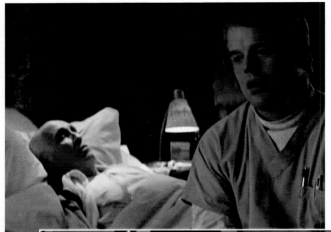

Left: Jason Robards and Philip Seymour Hoffman sing along to 'Wise Up' in the film *Magnolia*.

Below: The video for 'Save Me', featuring Tom Cruise and other cast members, was directed by Paul Thomas Anderson and shot on set during the making of *Magnolia*.

Left: A still from the promotional film for the track 'Video', from 2005's *The Forgotten Arm*. (*SuperEgo*)

Right: For 'Labrador', from the *Charmer* album from 2012, director Tom Scharpling recreated the 'Voices Carry' video, as featured in the first image of this photo section.

Above: Again from the video for 'Labrador', Michael Hausman returns on drums and Ted Leo is featured wearing a Robert Holmes-style hairpiece!

Right: In 2011, Aimee played herself in an episode of comedy show *Portlandia*, working a second job as a cleaner to make ends meet.

Left: *Lost in Space* from 2002 also appeared in a two-disc special edition, featuring ten additional tracks. (*SuperEgo*)

Right: The DVD cover for *Live at St. Ann's Warehouse*, an intimate record of Aimee and her band in concert. (*SuperEgo*)

Right: *The Forgotten Arm* from 2005, Aimee's first concept album, with cover painting by Owen Smith. (*SuperEgo*)

Left: The original cover of *One More Drifter in the Snow*, Aimee's Christmas album from 2006, which is a mix of traditional and new songs. (*SuperEgo*)

Above: Aimee playing 'I Should've Known' on BBC's *Later With Jools Holland* in 1993.

Right: *Live at St. Ann's Warehouse.* l to r: John Sands, Paul Bryan, Aimee, Julian Coryell.

Live at St. Ann's Warehouse. The band is as above, with keyboardist Jebin Bruni far left.

Right: Playing 'Labrador' live in 2012, with long-time collaborator Paul Bryan on bass.

Below: Performing as 'The Both' with Ted Leo in an NPR Music Tiny Desk Concert from 2014.

Playing 'You Never Loved Me' live in 2017 with Jonathan Coulton (far right), plus Chris Thile, Sara Watkins, Rich Dworsky, Alan Hampton and Ted Poor.

Left: *@#%&*! Smilers*, from 2008, with artwork by Gary Taxali, saw Aimee take her sound in a more keyboard-influenced direction. (*SuperEgo*)

Right: 2012's *Charmer* featured Ed Sherman's hypnotic graphic effects and a reintegration of guitars into the previous album's keyboard-orientated sound. (*SuperEgo*)

Above: Aimee and Ted Leo joined forces to form The Both in 2014. It was Aimee's first contribution to a band in 25 years. (*SuperEgo*)

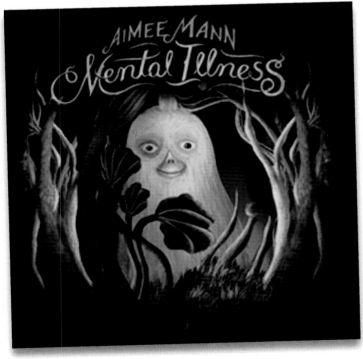

Left: 2017's *Mental Illness*, Aimee's latest and most acoustic-orientated album. It won her a Grammy for Best Folk Album. Surreal artwork is by Andrea Deszö. (*SuperEgo*)

Above: Aimee recording *Mental Illness* in 2016.

Below: From the *Making of Mental Illness* video, with added Mellotron.

Gail Marowitz came up with the pulp fiction feel, inspired by vintage novels, with Aimee re-writing the lyrics into prose. Smith produced a new painting for the cover, and images for each *chapter*, depicting not just boxing, but other events from the story. Regarding the characters' look, Smith said, 'The guy was easy – noir ex-boxer, tough. The woman, I thought, should be basically a strong person but with some vulnerability, like the good girl in a noir film, not the femme fatale. She should have qualities of Aimee, but not be her.' *The Forgotten Arm* went on to win a Grammy for Best Recording Package.

'It's a character study and a relationship study', Mann said to *Interview*, the story split into a series of vignettes, as she eavesdrops on events from John and Caroline's life. Usually, one to shy away from discipline in her writing, Aimee tried to stick with the storyline. 'I almost wish it was even more structured. Some of the songs are not even as specific to the story as I would have liked.' This is the first (and so far only) album in Aimee's catalogue which she has written alone with no collaborations. The tight musical unit confidently colours the light and shade amid deceptively simple arrangements.

Describing it as 'A dozen more odes to dysfunction', *Record Collector* highlighted how the dark and serious backdrop is lightened by Aimee's 'unerring grasp of melody', and skill as someone who 'knows her way around a witty couplet', concluding that 'You'll not hear many better records this year'.

In 2009, Mann announced that she was working with Paul Bryan on a musical based on *The Forgotten Arm*. But progress has been slow, continuing on and off over the years, with no news on a completed work to date.

'Dear John' (Mann) (3:07)

This solid rocker sets out the album as more straight-ahead, after the elaborate *Lost in Space*. The flourishing fanfare announces its presence before piano is pitched against sliding guitar phrases with upfront bass, in a spacious sound.

Caroline recalls first meeting John at the State Fair (depicted in Chapter One of the CD booklet) amid the sights and sounds of the fairground. She sees John's boxing exhibition rounds against local amateurs. He's 'Throwing kisses so Richmond's unfortunates can go on', pulling his punches rather than knocking them flat at the outset. It seems that Caroline's 'lectures' to the other girls to 'behave, While the band played all your favourite songs', were to warn them off, as she wanted him for herself.

The scene appears to jump back to John's draft and posting to Vietnam, where he may have been wounded, ending any hopes of a successful boxing career, leading to him scratching a living in boxing booths. The loss of his career, and sadness regarding his current state, are reflected in the song's title, the dreaded *Dear John* letter – being those received by soldiers to break off relationships that had sustained them – a probable catalyst for his drinking. Caroline appears to be looking back from the future, with fond memories of John and the Fair, the song thus filled with melancholy.

Aimee's voice is in laid-back rock mode, Jeff Trott contributing a soaring guitar solo with thumping rhythmic support. The extended repetition of the last line with organ, and the four-note figure on the final word ending in a long organ fade, is a great way to finish the striking opener.

'King Of The Jailhouse' (Mann) (5:19)

A song of 'bitterness, unhappiness and dysfunction', she told the audience onn *Live At St. Ann's Warehouse*. An old Cadillac heads cross-country, packed with possessions, its occupants hoping that 'sharing the burden will lighten the load'. The West End Horns make an impression as we eavesdrop, John ('The king of the jailhouse') driving, while Caroline ('The queen of the road'), sleeps in the back. There's a mournful tone from piano and bass, Aimee's weary vocal counting the drifting miles. John is realising that he's falling apart, but can only confess it to Caroline while she sleeps, the sound getting more intense as he begins. 'Baby, there's something wrong with me, That I can't see'. The low resonance of Jay Bellerose's drums beat out the pace.

Caroline seems to rouse from her slumber, or is he imagining her response. Sliding guitar and horns add an emotional impact as she notes that there are no right answers. 'You can't simply stand there and hope for the best'. She tells him to wake her when they reach Mexico, cryptically adding that she'll tell him 'a secret I don't even know'. Neither of them have any answers. He doesn't want to return to where they began, but if she has a secret, he needs to know what it is.

The horns come to a crescendo in the second chorus, taking a lead role through the bridge and the final chorus where the sound is more expansive. There's a blanket of sadness over this song – they need to fix what's wrong, but without being sure of the cause, they're running away from a situation they can't resolve. It's a vivid and atmospheric snapshot of a moment, the pair wandering aimlessly in a kind of limbo, the white lines of the road, sliding under the speeding car.

'Goodbye Caroline' (Mann) (3:53)

John convinces himself that his failures are hurting Caroline, and in Las Vegas ('Where it's lit day for night, And the clocks wear their faces bowed, Where the hands and cuffs gleam white, As they hang on a nicotine cloud') he decides to leave, believing it's for her own good. He intends to get help for his alcoholism but ultimately resists the treatment.

He urges her to get dressed, and he'll drop her at the bus depot. He acknowledges her belief in him, and describes her as 'my favourite faith healer', but his reliance on drink will only ever let her down. The booklet shows her standing forlornly outside the motel, suitcase in hand.

With jaunty acoustic guitar and driving drums, we're straight into the verse, Aimee's forthright vocal taking in a repetitive melody. The lovely chorus with piano and background organ, sees Jeff Trott's guitar coming into greater focus, taking in a short but effective solo. There's a positive direction. Despite the heartbreak for Caroline, decisions have been made and there's a greater feeling of intent as a result. The instrumental breakdown at the end is great, keys, bass and drums flying as the guitar solos above, slowing to an easy stop to fade on a single organ chord.

'Going Through The Motions' (Mann) (2:57)

Set a while later, Caroline confronts John about his drinking and disturbed mental state, a probable side-effect of the boxing. She wants him to come clean about the pain that's eating away at him. With 'Something isn't right!', we're straight into it. The rolling rhythm pushes along a mid-paced song, as Caroline confirms that she isn't buying his 'dog and pony show' declarations that he's better now and won't let drinking take over again. Spiky guitars and resonant drums add interesting sidelines as she senses that things will soon go badly wrong. He's 'only going through the motions' of getting his life turned around. Her concern is palpable:

Feel like I'm in jail
With you and Mr Hyde
A guy who leaves a trail
About a mile wide

His elaborate pleas to convince her otherwise, fall on deaf ears. She's heard it all before and is cynical about the 'big parade' that he'll expect for every day he stays clean, sadly noting that 'when the trumpets fade, You'll go under like a submarine', back into the depths of his addiction. He lacks awareness and 'won't see it coming'. She's offering him a brighter future, but he's going to blow it, and she's fed up with his attempts coming to nothing. There's a care-worn resignation in 'But baby, I'm afraid I'll never see you well', the 'big finale' that this is all leading to, most likely his demise. In the booklet, she's pictured on the telephone to him, dishevelled and in anguish. It's a very strong *Caroline* song.

'I Can't Get My Head Around It' (Mann) (3:37)

John admits that he has tried to compensate for his problems and has resisted treatment, which has only made his issues, and frustration at being unable to make it in boxing, worse.

This seems to come from her perspective, the 'I want to believe' lines in response to his upbeat patter from the previous song. However, the booklet depicts him confessing his problems to a therapist, so it's probable that the protagonist changes during the song.

Bryan's plucked bass intro with acoustic guitar, leads into a heart-rending vocal. She wants to believe him, but she can't, and doesn't understand why he's doing it, his words undermining things, making it more difficult to resolve. She wants to believe it when he says 'Baby, I'm dry', but it's all in vain – 'And I'll pour the drinks, Like a true believer'. Her dismay at his drinking is acute in the next verse:

> Like, way more real than real
> The world inside the glass
> That struggles to conceal
> The wreckage on the overpass

His reality when drinking is more vivid to him than the actuality that appears to her – she can see the wreckage that he is oblivious to. Piano becomes a key feature, adding an engaging side melody to the laid-back chorus, as the frustration feeds through in the supplementary section and through the bridge.

'She Really Wants You' (Mann) (3:26)

Mid-tempo with bass upfront, keening electric guitar and organ drive it into a sunny vocal that confounds the situation as John hits rock bottom. He has moved in with his father while finally tackling his addiction, but Caroline just wants him back, despite all his faults.

It's a third-party perspective, as if that of a friend, watching as John sits in his pyjamas in the basement (as in the booklet), waiting for her to call. She makes up an excuse to visit him, but he doesn't feel anything, 'Tired of all the dramas, maybe'. The chorus implores him to keep working to dispel his demons, because 'she really wants you', and as soon as he realises that, 'I'm sure you'd come running, baby'.

The second verse seems to be set later. He is packing to move in with her, but he wonders to himself, 'What made you choose her?'. He notes that 'moving house when you're a stoner' can mean that 'Everything you come across, Makes you feel like such a loser'. By the third verse, it appears that he has decided that she is just another habit that he needs to break – 'the stray that you found, That looked so cute at the pound, Now has you putting her down as rabid'.

Again, the bridge ramps up the instrumentation, followed by an extended guitar solo. Organ sings throughout, drums keeping things moving.

It's a sad point in the story. It seems that their relationship has run its course and is dead and buried, his problems preventing any potential future. A sorry twist in the tale.

'Video' (Mann) (3:35)

Later, John professes his love for Caroline, but there's another layer of pain as he reveals his depression. The ominous funereal drumbeat and piano line hold a relentless, repetitive grind, like someone drowning as life gets the better of them. Aimee's vocal is subdued, John telling of a sadness like being 'stuck in a cone of silence, Like a big balloon with nothing but ballast'. 'Drink me down, or I'll drown in a sea of giants' suggests an *Alice in Wonderland* shrinking potion, his depression taking hold as he wastes away from reality. He implores Caroline to tell him she loves him as the vocal opens out into the chorus, his pain mixing with 'nonstop memories of you' and 'loops of seven-hour kisses', as if in a video. He can't understand why he feels so low. He has saved some money from boxing, but that can't buy happiness, and his physical health is making him fragile:

> Like a building that's been slated for blasting
> I'm the proof that nothing is lasting
> Counting to eleven as it collapses

The booklet image – the only one in colour – is striking. John sits in his corner between rounds, seemingly dejected and spent, his trainer trying to build him up for one more round.

Jeff Trott's mandolin adds a different texture, with drums muffled throughout. The emotion comes through as Aimee sings the outro, shot through with John's pain: 'Baby, Baby, I love you, But baby, I feel so bad'. It's one of the most moving and beautiful depictions of depression I've ever heard. The promo film is a simple matter of Aimee singing the song to camera with acoustic guitar, amid starlight and multi-image effects.

'Little Bombs' (Mann) (3:49)

Hotel life in Atlanta, looking down from the 22nd floor at the scene below. 'While perspective lines converge, Rows of cars and buses merge'. The imagery is ripe and vivid:

> All the sweet green trees of Atlanta burst
> Like little bombs
> Or little pom-poms
> Shaken by a careless hand
> That dries them off
> And leaves again

The next verse exemplifies the relationship fizzling out, ending with a whimper rather than a bang:

> Life just kind of empties out
> Less a deluge than a drought
> Less a giant mushroom cloud
> Than an unexploded shell
> Inside a cell
> Of the Lennox Hotel

The Lennox could be the one near Boston's Charles River. John is shown in a cheap hotel room, alone. It appears that the pair are now distanced – one in Atlanta, the other in Boston – still victims of the dreams of a life they thought they'd enjoy together. The meaning is ambiguous, but it's a beautiful song and probably the finest on the album. It's a key moment in the story that describes the sadness of being alone, even when viewing the hustle and bustle of life in a busy street scene, as an observer rather than an active participant. Whoever the protagonist, we have to guess at the contents of the 'notice on my door' – possibly a request for John to leave, 'While outside, The sun is shining on'.

There's resignation in not being happy with your lot but being unable to do much about it. The backing is delicate, lightly strummed acoustic complemented by electric accents, piano and skittering brushed drums. There's a dreamy feel to the vocal, indicative of a detached view of life. A class song through and through.

'That's How I Knew This Story Would Break My Heart' (Mann) (4:19)

Caroline speaks of her undying love for John, whilst drawing his picture. She imagines the picture he would draw to be a bird with a fear that cannot be tamed, even within the 'cage' of a relationship, the chanticleer (rooster) an analogy which suggests his boxer's demeanour. The booklet shows a dejected Caroline leaning against her dressing table, alone, the chorus painting its own picture. 'That's how I knew this story would break my heart, When you wrote it'. The second verse is particularly sad, but hauntingly beautiful:

> So, like a ghost in the snow
> I'm getting ready to go
> 'Cause baby, that's all I know
> How to open the door
> And though the exit is crude
> It saves me coming unglued
> For when you're not in the mood
> For the gloves and the canvas floor

John's depression is dragging her down; she's helpless to do anything about it and must leave for her own survival. The exit is there; she just has to use it.

Largely featuring Jebin Bruni's soulful piano, it's a particularly emotional song, slow and sad as Aimee intones the words, as Caroline to herself. Backing vocals accentuate at key points, Chamberlin voicings adding to the melancholy air. The bass is sparse and there's very little additional instrumentation as the song builds in a stately fashion. The more upbeat final chorus adds drums and electric guitar, but its nature remains solemn, the repeated chord sequence after the final words, a complete joy.

'I Can't Help You Anymore' (Mann) (4:52)

The image shows the pair, seemingly during an argument, the words initially looking back to their meeting at the fairground. But after the trials and tribulations they have endured, Caroline's faith breaks and she can no longer 'keep Pandora's boxes shut', sadly aware that 'I'll fail you badly when you really need me'. The chorus underlines her desperate position:

'Cause I don't know
What I should know
That I can't help you anymore

She can't make a happy ending of the story they've written together, and asks:

Was I the bullet or the gun
Or just a target drawn upon
A wall that you decided
Wasn't worth defending?

It's heartrending stuff – the repetition of 'I can't help you anymore', and the lack of self-worth in 'look what I have done, The ruins just go on and on, I've got to let it go now, Or it will drag me under'.

It's another song with a sense of purpose, Caroline deciding that things have to end. The introductory acoustic guitar is joined by electric, over a subtly-pounding drums and bass rhythm. The vocal is subdued to start, building into the stubbornly forthright chorus as the instrumentation swells. Piano takes a more prominent role in the second verse, guitar soaring over the bridge as frustration boils over. Julian Coryell adds plaintive keyboard to the outro as guitar continues to solo through the extended instrumental break.

'I Was Thinking I Could Clean Up for Christmas' (Mann) (4:23)

Honky-tonk piano is forceful right out of the gate with John's hopeful words. His attitude is positive, but his comment to Caroline that 'I was thinking I could clean up for Christmas, And then, baby, I'm through' smacks of delusion. It seems that Christmas is only four weeks away, an insignificant timespan 'that couldn't make any difference, except maybe to you'. He's going cold-turkey, and using the thought of a wonderful fairytale Christmas as his inspiration: 'One less fucker trying to get in the business of the prodigal son'.

Record Collector called it 'A toe-tapping anthem to hope and redemption'. There's uplifting energy as the rhythm picks up into the chorus, John's positivity almost palpable. The image shows him on Skid Row, but he is resolutely confident that he can turn his back on the drink. 'I can't live loaded and I can't live sober', his dilemma put in sharp focus. Once he's clean, will he be able to stay that way?

The last verse takes in an apology that he intends to give Caroline when Christmas arrives, drums almost adding a heartbeat underneath: 'I'm sorry that I made you a witness to my moral decay ... Once upon a time I believed it was a victimless crime'. It builds beautifully, and by this point is swinging quite seductively, with wailing organs in the rocking finish. The listener is on John's side, hopeful he can pull it off and save the day for both of them.

'Beautiful' (Mann) (3:48)

In this final track, we rejoin John and Caroline after what seems to be a long absence. Against the odds, and with Caroline's help, John has managed to get over his alcoholism. Does she truly believe that he's cured, or is she just turning a blind eye to some of his indiscretions as her love for him is so strong? Either way, it's something of an unexpected happy ending.

With a piano crash intro, the rolling rhythm kicks in with stabs of piano and guitar. John's now driving an Eldorado. He pulls up at her place and they kiss 'with some bravado'. She's taking photographs again, happy that they're of him. As they drive, she remarks how 'It's scary when it's so beautiful', something that they haven't experienced much of in their time together. The chorus is a release of pent-up emotion on sustained guitar chords. Her love for him is clear, as it has been throughout their story:

> 'Cause I can't even stand it
> 'Cause I don't want to end it
> To be perfectly candid
> Baby, you're beautiful

But she wishes he could see it in himself. There's a relaxed and loving vibe in the bridge: 'All I have to do today is make you happy, The only thing you have to say is, "It's all lovely, baby"'. They check into a hotel, the chapter image showing them in bed together, seemingly reconciled and content with their lot. She photographs him again. 'Baby, I'm dazzled by the view'; 'You don't need to tell me, I'm completely powerless'; 'I wish you could see it too, Baby, how I see you'. But there still seem to be some secrets.

And so, the story ends. It's been a hell of a ride, but they seem to have found a way to make it work.

Related tracks
'Who Knows' (Mann) (1:00)

This short bonus track for the Japanese release casts doubt on the happy ending suggested by 'Beautiful', in typical Aimee style. Unsurprisingly – given John's personality and the nature of their relationship – in this brief epilogue, Caroline admits that things could still go either way and she doesn't know what the future will hold for them. 'He's always pulled through before, but that's no comfort now, Who knows in a holy war, what's winning anyhow?'.

Damn it!

One More Drifter In The Snow (2006)

Personnel:
Aimee Mann: Vocals, Acoustic Guitar
Jay Bellerose: Drums and Percussion
Paul Bryan: Bass Guitar, Background Vocals
Chris Bruce: Acoustic Guitar
Duke Levine: Banjo, Electric Guitar, Mandola
Patrick Warren: Celeste, Chamberlin, Keyboards, Piano, Pump Organ
Grant-Lee Phillips: Vocals
Producer: Paul Bryan
Record Label: SuperEgo
Recorded: May to August 2006
Released: 31 October 2006
Running Time: 33:05
Highest chart place: US:-, UK:-

Not many people would have expected a Christmas album from Aimee
Mann, but towards the end of 2006, *One More Drifter in the Snow* appeared.
Recording began in May, but, she told *Billboard*:

> It didn't take any time to (get) into the Christmas vibe... before it got really
> hot, it was just so nice to be in the mood, without the pressures of buying
> presents and stuff'.

Comprising a selection of classic Christmas songs plus two originals, Mann
cited Johnny Mathis' 1958 *Merry Christmas* as an influence, deciding to
eschew her regular style or the 'groovy modern Christmas record' route, in
favour of something more 'Mel Tormé, Dean Martin, Frank Sinatra, lounge-y,
sort of Julie London'. She was also inspired by the soundtrack to 1965's *A
Charlie Brown Christmas* by the Vince Guaraldi Trio, liking that it had 'a lot
of dark and mysterious undertones. First, Charlie Brown is depressed by the
commercialism of Christmas, and then there's Linus, who steps out to tell the
story of the nativity, with this heartbreakingly moral stance. We wanted our take
to be all that – mysterious, quiet, moody. And classy'.

Rolling Stone described the result as 'forlorn. This isn't a cup of holiday
cheer – it's the bracing chaser'.

For the first time, Aimee released songs co-written with Michael Penn. When
asked about them writing as a couple, she said:

> We don't really collaborate, mostly because we both like to work in the same
> style. Also, Michael has a harmonic sensibility that's totally different from mine.
> He just goes to chord changes that are kind of foreign to me. It's hard when
> you're writing with someone, and he's going to this chord change and you're
> thinking, 'Wow, I would never go there.'

Regarding the exchange of ideas, she said:

> Every now and then there'll be a song that he's working on that'll be close
> enough to my style of writing, that I'll come in and say, 'Look, why don't you
> try this chord progression?' or, 'Why don't you do this thing in the middle?'.
> And he'll give me advice as well, particularly if I'm stuck. I might ask him what
> he thinks and he'll come up with some chord that I hadn't thought of. But in
> general, I don't think we really click as writers.

'Whatever Happened To Christmas?' (Jimmy Webb) (2:52)

Jimmy Webb's song, previously recorded by Frank Sinatra in 1968. *Rolling
Stone* noted that Aimee 'makes the notion of walking in a winter wonderland
sound lonely and cold', but that's not particularly fair as it was a sad song in
the first place. Aimee adds a twangy guitar in place of Frank's orchestration, her
voice crisp and warm as she beautifully delivers a nostalgic view of Christmases
past, that will either make you feel sad or cosy, depending on your point of
view. It's something of a lesser-known Christmas song and good to hear.

'The Christmas Song (Chestnuts Roasting On An Open Fire)' (Mel Tormé, Bob Wells) (3:19)

First released by Nat King Cole in 1946, it doesn't get much more Christmassy
than this. Aimee recorded it as early as 1991 (for a Boston compilation),
releasing it as a single in 2000. The piano and bass intro moves on brushed
drums and light jazz guitar, with subtle harmonium orchestration. As delicate
as a fresh dusting of snow, Aimee's voice suits it – as traditional as you can get,
albeit with a fresh coat of paint. With a tail-off of 'Auld Lang Syne', if it doesn't
make you wish for Christmas, there's something wrong with you.

'Christmastime' (Michael Penn) (3:18)

There's an *old time* feel, with scratchy guitar, banjo and piano giving bluesy
and rustic folk textures. Aimee sings nicely, but it isn't the most satisfying song.
The sentiment, however, is positive and warm. The iTunes release replaced
it with a not very festive 'Clean Up for Christmas' (from *The Forgotten Arm*)
and a cover of Joni Mitchell's 'River'. The version of 'Christmastime' recorded
with Penn for Paul Thomas Anderson's *Hard Eight* in 1996, is more satisfying,
as they sing alternate lines, duetting some, that setting working better with a
more orchestrated feel.

'I'll Be Home For Christmas' (Kim Gannon, Walter Kent) (3:18)

First recorded by Bing Crosby in 1943, originally from the perspective of a soldier
away at the front. Aimee's version features strings and an incongruous, almost
Hawaiian, guitar. She sings warmly over the shuffling rhythm with twinkling
percussion, and the guitar is actually the clincher, giving a sunny warmth which

works well against the sleigh bells. *Rolling Stone* noted that 'for all its loving invocation of snow and mistletoe, (it's) one of the saddest Christmas songs ever'.

'You're A Mean One, Mr. Grinch' (Theodor Geisel, Albert Hague) (3:27)
With acoustic guitar from Chris Bruce and guest vocals from Grant Lee Phillips (hamming it up in Seuss style), Aimee gets in the swing for a fun version that just might not be fun enough. However, it's a nice diversion, unexpectedly quirky, whilst not entirely convincing.

'Winter Wonderland' (Felix Bernard, Richard B. Smith) (3:46)
Chris Bruce's guitar adds a country sheen, and you can't get a more traditional Christmas song than this. The rhythm is basic, the fun side of the season shining through as Aimee croons beautifully. Things fall away for a section lightly supported by strings and guitar with percussion just where it's needed. Bruce's solo at the end makes this the twangiest Christmas song you're likely to hear.

'Have Yourself A Merry Little Christmas' (Hugh Martin, Ralph Blane) (3:54)
Another classic, the arrangement again goes for a country-folk feel, with sweeping orchestral backing. Aimee's singing is lovely, piano supporting with bell percussion and a warm, homely vibe. Aquatic keyboards add a different touch, and it's a fine version of a song that underpins many people's thoughts of what a traditional Christmas is about.

'God Rest Ye Merry Gentlemen' (Traditional) (2:06)
A proper Christmas carol with a particularly effective brass arrangement, as Aimee delivers this staple of Salvation Army bands in every town during the season. The arrangement is opened up with low voices, guitar, sleigh bells and chiming keyboards, but at its heart, it's about the voice and brass. This is the full seven-verse version based on W. B. Sandys' 1833 collection *Christmas Carols Ancient and Modern*.

'White Christmas' (Irving Berlin) (2:58)
This song *is* Christmas, selling over 100,000,000 copies in all versions (half being of Bing Crosby's original 1942 recording). Countrified guitar again features, Aimee singing breathlessly with simple percussion. There's plenty of space, and it's as bare and chilly as icicles on a pine tree (rather than gathered together around an open hearth), but it is quite beautiful.

'Calling On Mary' (Aimee Mann, Michael Penn, Paul Bryan) (4:02)
A full band song in more traditional Mann style, and it's cracking, the pace easy with the repeated refrain of 'Merry Christmas, Merry Christmas' alternating

through the verses. It smacks of sidewalk Santas and 'Salvation coming, cheap today', in a song of loneliness and lost love, of searching 'the skyline for a star ... And baby I wondered where you are'. The line 'Comfort's not possible when you look past the joy to the end', is classic Mann, and calling on Mary does not help as 'She offered sight to the blind, But I'm not the miracle kind'. The song, and a very pleasant album, ends with:

And to all the lost souls down below

What's one more drifter in the snow?
Merry Christmas, Merry Christmas

If there's a star above, then it can look like love
When they light up the Christmas tree

Related Tracks
'River' (Joni Mitchell) (4:00)
Added to the iTunes release, it also appeared as a bonus on the UK reissue in November 2008, which came in an alternative sleeve – Aimee looking sad, clutching a couple of Santa Claus figures. Aimee stays true to Joni Mitchell's original, and it's a fine addition, retaining the purity of Joni's version, the voice accompanied by piano alone in the first half, Aimee utilising her full range. Later, the arrangement builds with sleigh bells accenting the wintery feel. A great song in any version, this one does it no disservice.

@#%&*! Smilers (2008)

Personnel:
Aimee Mann: Vocals, Acoustic and Bowed Guitars
Paul Bryan: Bass Guitar, Backing Vocals, Horn Arrangements
Jay Bellerose: Drums
Jamie Edwards: Keyboards
Buddy Judge, Kimon Kirk, Sean Hayes: Backing Vocals
Jebin Bruni: Moog
Dave Eggers: Whistling
Patrick Warren: String Arrangements
Willie Murillo: Trumpet
Mark Visher: Tenor and Baritone Saxophone
Jason Thor: Trombone and Bass Trombone
Eric Gorfain, Daphne Chen, Amy Wickman, Alyssa Park, Terry Glenny, Marisa
Kuney, Melisa Reiner: Violins
Leah Katz, Caroline Buckman, David Sage: Violas
Richard Dodd, Alan Matthews, John Krovaza: Cellos
Producer: Paul Bryan
Record Label: SuperEgo
Recorded: The Sound Factory, Hollywood, CA
Released: 2 June 2008
Running Time: 45:51
Highest chart place: US:32, UK:-

In 2007, concerned about the scale of illegal downloading and file sharing, Aimee lent her name to the Artists Against Piracy group. She was asked to write a song for the *Shrek 3* movie, to convey Shrek's 'You can do it!' optimism – 'Not really my speciality!'. It was a less than enjoyable experience, as she told *Rock 'n' Reel*: 'They kept coming back to me, asking me to change this and change that. It was like being in a record company. It was maddening. It got to the point where I was hoping they wouldn't take it'. She noted wryly that the last straw was the studio's request to 'Make it sound more like Fallout Boy'!

My policy for writing songs for movies is, 'I'll give it a try'. It's not about chasing the dollar. And I did happen to write a song that I thought fitted really well. But after three or four times going back into the studio, it was becoming a drag. I was relieved (when it didn't make the finished movie). It felt so uncomfortable.

Aimee told *Billboard* that her next album would be a departure from *The Forgotten Arm*.

I've been writing more on the piano, just so I don't get into a rut. When I write on the guitar, my fingers tend to move to the same chord progressions.

There's no electric guitar at all, which you weirdly don't miss. It's kind of this all-keyboard situation, which is great. It's an interesting amalgamation of sounds.

She confirmed to *Dcist* that there is no concept to *@#%&*! Smilers* other than 'just to have each song be as different as it wants to be, and not worry about any kind of through-line. The through-line is really just the vibe of the instrumentation and the production and the musicians. We recorded it pretty much live'.

Regarding the title, 'I'd read this article about some study somebody did about the kinds of images people respond to. Most people respond to human faces. But apparently, across cultural lines, everybody responds most positively to a smiling cartoon face'. This reminded her of an early internet newsgroup called *alt.bitter*, and someone complaining about the 'fucking smilers' who would approach him at work when he was in a bad mood, and try to cheer him up.

A limited-edition book featured illustrations by Toronto-based artist, Gary Taxali, gaining another Grammy nomination for its packaging. Taxali attended the release at an L.A. gallery. 'It was then I really got to appreciate the finished product by seeing people's reaction for the first time.'

Aimee noted of the cartoon elements to *Varoom*:

It's very graphic, it's a little collage-y. I felt like Gary's work fit in with the sound of the record and the kind of language I used. It was brighter, more orangey! He printed silkscreen on top of older paper, which to me makes sense, having in the music a kind of organic acoustic sound in the rhythm section, but on top you've got Moog and clavinet.

Taxali listened to the songs, and they talked about them before he started sketching. Some of Mann's doodles were included in three of the finished images, but he isn't saying which. Taxali found the project's emphasis on 'exquisite design and exquisite printing' very rewarding – 'Something that no record company does anymore'.

Reviews were favourable, *Billboard* stating it 'pops with colour, something that gives it an immediacy that's rare for an artist known for songs that subtly worm their way into the subconscious' and 'There are both big pop hooks and a rich sonic sheen', while *The Boston Globe* noted 'tunes that seep into your brain with the stealth of Mann's own beguiling murmur'.

'Freeway' (Mann) (3:50)

The video for this single sees Aimee seated, as a couple dance behind her. Split-screen effects break things up before she joins in with some of their moves at the end.

She stated in an interview with *Newsweek* that the inspiration was a friend with plenty of money but a bad amphetamine habit, who cruised Interstate 5 to feed his addiction. '(He) was living in Los Angeles, going down to Orange County and talking doctors into prescribing him speed, because he was charming and had money. It's well and good to have a lot of money, but you can't really afford to have that much money, because it enables you to slowly kill yourself.'

The first verse sets the scene, culminating in 'They'll sell you all the speed you want if you can take the blackmail'. The second verse ramps up the cynicism:

You found yourself a prophet
But you left him on the boardwalk
Another chocolate Easter bunny
Hollowed out by your talk

A light buzz of guitars and bass opens with skittering drums, all coming together with piano, as the basic quartet kick into the excellent hooky chorus. It's a great opener, cool and pumping, vintage keyboards filling it out and setting the tone for the album. Aimee starts in diffident mood, getting more powerful as the song builds, closing with a nice keyboard and drums outro. An acoustic version appeared as a bonus on the iTunes release, the video included on the Japanese edition.

'Stranger Into Starman' (Mann) (1:31)
When asked if this song reflected the cult of celebrity, Aimee said, 'It's more about the general idea of elevating people in your estimation that don't deserve it, based on how they appear, rather than how they are. You could call it narcissism'.

Two verses and a brief chorus, this is one of her shortest songs. But it packs a punch as 'Stranger' is turned into 'Starman in the Sunday *New York Times*'. Starting with vocal alone, joined by upright piano, Pulitzer Prize-winning American poet, Anne Sexton, is namechecked. Her confessional poems describe long battles with depression, suicidal tendencies and intimate details of her private life, so it's not surprising that her work appeals to Aimee. Sexton loved the palindrome 'Rats live on no evil star', hence the line 'Anne Sexton's star rats'. (As an aside, Peter Gabriel dedicated his song 'Mercy Street' to Sexton). The line 'Working backwards 'til it rhymes' points out the palindrome simile, but also relates to the process of making sense of the person put on a pedestal in the real world, and finding them wanting.

Strings come in for the repeated chorus line 'For the love of God you can't tell me again'. Aimee sings the frustration beautifully, before becoming more prominent in the second verse as she imposes the true reality: 'With a pencil and eraser I've rewritten all your crimes'. Vintage keyboards add colour to this brief but arresting piece.

'Looking For Nothing' (Mann) (3:46)

Who is Macka? Why is he keen to ride on the Mouse and the Tilt-a-Whirl? Canada is apparently looking for a smile from a pin-up girl, while everyone else is waiting for something they can pin all their feelings on. But not Aimee, she 'ain't looking for nothing, Just spend the money I made, I ain't gotta do nothing today'.

> I got high on the Ferris wheel
> Didn't like how it made me feel
> So alone
> Another cog in the loading zone

She's not looking for trouble, money, or thrills, ''Cause when you're looking for nothing, Baby, it's not the speed that kills'. But what of Macka and Canada?

> Macka went on home when the fireworks and rides were done
> Canada got busted with a girl who was way too young

Jamie Edwards' sad electric piano, leads here, organ accents adding to the melancholic setting of bass, drums and guitar. There's a nice piano solo after the bridge, and a real feeling of space in the easy pacing, with more energy in the final chorus. It's an enjoyably mellow listen.

'Phoenix' (Mann) (3:56)

A strident piano moves into acoustic guitar, and you can feel the heat of the desert, but rhyming 'Phoenix' with 'Kleenex' is a bit wince-inducing! It seems she's making a lucky escape from a town of javelinas (another name for peccaries) and 'Driving Under the Influence'. She may be sad to be leaving him, but piano and strings swell behind the directness of the chorus as she explains:

> You love me like a dollar bill
> You roll me up and trade me in
> And if you had the chance you will
> And if you get the chance again

Patrick Warren's string arrangement is lush and warm as the song moves to a more elegiac place, with real emotion in the bridge. There's consideration of when the decision to run should be made – 'balance heartache with your fun, And when the scales tip, You know you're done', as 'Love doesn't change a thing'. When the game is effectively up, there's no benefit in extra time. An acoustic version appeared as B-side of '31 Today'.

'Borrowing Time' (Mann) (3:12)

At a 2017 concert, Aimee introduced this as 'a song about not letting life just happen to you', mentioning that it was inspired by Snow White, although

Sleeping Beauty also features. Starting as the project for *Shrek 3*, she liked what she had written, and reworked it based on Grimm's fairy tales, 'So now it's like this weird, creepy, dark song. I was really glad to take the song back and do something that I was proud of'.

Stomping bass and a high keyboard melody usher us in. The protagonist lies asleep. The song urges her to get up – she's in danger and on borrowed time. Aimee is insistent, brass and backing vocals stressing the urgency. Of the question asked of the mirror, 'Alas, no answer could be clearer', but luckily, 'A substitute heart has just reprieved you', thanks to the huntsman's compassion. There's still danger: 'Beware, for flattering ruses have deceived you' – Aimee stepping out of the fairytale as the real world creeps in:

I don't want anything anyway
I was happy with what I had yesterday
Who wants the whole weight of the world
When it'll drag you down
Underground?

Brass fanfares as 'She's bringing the poison apple to ya, Sun's up and reveille's playing'. The layers of Jamie Edwards' keyboards with Jebin Bruni's Moog and Paul Bryan's brass arrangement, are very effective, and this is the fullest sound on the album. A particularly snappy number and certainly a highlight.

'It's Over' (Mann) (3:58)

A change of pace, starting gorgeously with sunny piano and Aimee in positive voice. 'Everything's beautiful, Every day's a holiday, The day you live without it'. But, 'Everything shifts and falls unless you care about it', and as the title suggests, it isn't going to last as doubts set in, strings carrying the emotion:

You sit there in the darkness
And you make plans but they're hopeless
And you blame God when you're lonely
And you'll call it fate when you show up too late and it's over

It seems that she speaks of someone else. 'You were the golden boy, A mix of brains and muscle ... not just another hustle'. It's another song of seizing the day and taking action to get what you wish for:

'Cause nothing can wait forever
They don't give unlimited chances in life
They hand you the knife and tell you to cut it around

A light drum-beat picks up with this second verse, piano taking up most of the rhythm as strings sing sweetly. 'Let's fly', she cries, as the strings lift powerfully.

'Baby let's ride' as the 'days are getting shorter', but it seems that her urging is in vain. Once again, kudos to Patrick Warren for his string arrangement. A beautiful song of true depth.

'31 Today' (Mann) (4:52)

Released ahead of the album in 2007, the video (directed by Bobcat Goldthwait and included on the Japanese release) sees Aimee sitting and strumming her guitar, trying to get through the song, while comedian Morgan Murphy larks around to put her off (including by affixing a moustache to her as she sings. Aimee actually looks great with it!)

Aimee confirmed to *The Independent* that it 'is about me, but I was also thinking about people I knew back then – "Getting loaded watching CNN". There was a guy I went out with for a while who was a musician and had a trust fund, so that's all he did. You can kid yourself that you're staying informed, but really'.

'I thought my life would be different somehow, I thought my life would be better by now, But it's not, and I don't know where to turn' describes the disappointment of many in the 20 to 40 age range who focus too much on themselves, including Aimee herself at that time in her life. 'Drinking Guinness in the afternoon, Taking shelter in the black cocoon' – birthdays being a time to examine where you are in life, and compare your achievements to those of others. There's ennui as she goes through the motions of a life seemingly going nowhere and already half-way done.

Called some guy I knew
Had a drink or two
And we fumbled as the day grew dark
I pretended that I felt a spark

The repeating keyboard riff is the prime musical element, picking up from the start and continuing at intervals throughout. Bass and electric piano make strong contributions, Mann's tone warm and comforting in the verse, building an almost angry edge for the chorus. It's a strong song that carries you along on its easy wave.

'The Great Beyond' (Mann) (3:12)

Aimee's contribution to the *National Geographic* wildlife movie *Arctic Tale*. Although it didn't feature in the finished film, it fits well with the thematic life cycles of walruses and polar bears, and their need to keep moving to avoid dangers both natural and man-made. The repeating phrase 'Go, honey go', into 'the great beyond', supports the mothers' quest to protect their offspring. With 'you can hide away for when everything goes wrong' and the need to move 'away from people who never treat you like they should', there's sound advice not to fight back, as 'every win is the beginning of defeat'.

The acoustic nature of the song ties in guitar and bass with wintery keyboard lines and evocative backing vocals from Paul Bryan. Aimee's voice is warm and comforting, showing concern, a steady forward-motion projected by the lilting rhythm. The bridge echos the piano-fuelled intro with:

In the woods or in the ice and snow
Where there is no one else you know
You've really nowhere else to go
So honey go

There's a fragile quality but with a determination to prevail, and it works well in the framework of the album. An acoustic version was a bonus with the iTunes release.

'Medicine Wheel' (Mann, Gretchen Seichrist) (4:08)
The only collaboration to date between Aimee and her half-sister Gretchen Seichrist, who provided poems for Mann to put to music. It's a rough ride right from the opening verse:

The day you left and you called me 'bitch'
I called you selfish
Better pull that switch
Put my son on amphetamines

Named for the symbolic Native American construction of stones growing out from a central spoke (here in a more urban setting, drawn on cardboard with a black marker), it's a song of healing, for the self, but also for a son in the face of a hard breakup. There's sadness, but strength, and also anger – the song showing character and charm as the drug-related activities of the woman's partner put her son in danger.

She reminds herself that by ending things, she 'did the right thing', as his constant lying and cheating drove her to distraction. 'You shade the truth almost every day, Phone calls at night, "It's gonna be okay" ... Everything that's good, you steal, From me'. She's unsure what he's up to, day or night. But the chorus may also be aimed at the son, who could be descending further into a world of addiction, the partner's 'words of encouragement' ultimately having the same effect as the drugs he peddles, sung with biting sarcasm in the phrasing.

The 'smooth blue pill' might refer to Ritalin, used to treat the boy's ADHD, where encouragement and a positive attitude would be equally positive. There are evocative lines like ''Cause once you were like a walking heart, Breaking in motion through the parking lot', as she looks back to earlier times, but the appeal of the partner's bad-boy deeds has now waned. She ponders on whether he can change, but she doesn't sound hopeful. Although this verse could also be directed at the son, hoping that he'll realise where his life is going and call for help:

> Maybe you'll wake up in jail alone
> And hold the handle of the one payphone
> And do the right thing

It's not a straightforward song, taking in anger at the wilful neglect of the partner and a call for the rehabilitation of the son. The lyric circles around, the lost tooth of the first verse coming back in the second, the words striking a different tone than most of Aimee's songs. But the music makes it a perfect fit, from the stately piano intro against which the words are starkly set. The instrumentation remains basic until the second verse, where drums, horns and bass pick things up, the words accentuated with backing vocals. Horns build to support the electric piano solo into the final repeat of the chorus, before returning to the simple piano and voice setting with a flourish in the last few lines. It's a beautifully structured song, a definite album highlight.

'Columbus Avenue' (Mann) (4:06)

From the delicate acoustic guitar count-in, there's a lazy pace with sparse piano and bass. Strings appear in the second verse, expanding into the chorus with drums, which become more forthright in the third. The bridge is a lovely, if sad, diversion before the final verse and chorus, Aimee's voice becoming more assertive. It's an elegant song that evolves gracefully before returning to lone acoustic guitar for the final lines.

It's set on the street in San Francisco, amid the storefronts and streetcars, taking in garish tattoo parlours, street entertainers, and asking 'What is Columbus Avenue to you now?':

> The place where you failed
> To make your story go over
> The place where you bailed
> And let the bottom drag you under

It seems that the object of the song moved down from Canada after a bout of paranoia, to San Francisco, 'Where you moved with a ghastly precision, To the echoes of bones in the air, Finding hope in an X-ray division, Of a world that's not there'. It's a cryptic song of annoyance at 'café sinners' and always having 'empty pockets', so it appears to concern someone down on their luck, possibly suffering from mental issues. Have they moved on? If so, maybe the song is a reminder of where they were and shows comfort in how they managed to turn themselves around once before. An 'Acoustic Trio Version' appeared on the Japanese release.

'Little Tornado' (Mann) (3:23)

After the piquant delicacy of 'Columbus Avenue', 'Little Tornado' also takes a diffident route, as a dark song with evocative words. The tornado seems to be localised. This 'bane of the trailer park' could be an individual, a partner, or a child creating havoc wherever they go. The disruptive nature comes through in 'Noah can build his ark, But he will never disembark' – you can try and escape but the ferocity of the storm will overwhelm you.

Acoustic guitar and scratchy violins forge an eerie setting. It's deceptively simple with a strong vocal, sporadic percussion and piano subtly building the tension. Youthful 'Go faster' exuberance comes through in the chorus, possibly hinting at the excitement of a relationship as it commences, the destructive elements only coming into focus later. The skilful juxtaposition of 'oh no' and 'don't know' in the haunting final words, suggest a trip into the unknown, made more sinister by echoed supporting voices and sombre whistling (by author Dave Eggers):

Oh no, no, we don't

No, we don't know

The involvement of Eggers could put new meaning into the song, his first book being a fictionalised memoir of quitting university to raise a younger sibling, after the death of both parents ripped through their lives like the tornado of the song.

'True Believer' (Mann, Grant Lee Phillips) (3:32)

There's a ghostly air as Aimee accompanies herself on acoustic guitar in the intro. A séance forms the analogy, its spirit visitors portraying a wayward partner returning home to the scene of his crimes. 'It's uncanny how you hover in the air, Of the wreckage that you left behind'. The chorus underlines the metaphor:

I want you but you're a poltergeist
I want you but, baby, the price is high
I want you and now I've said it twice
So Mary, dim the lights

His frustrating mixture of reality and illusion is all too clear, as with the fakery of the séance, where the art is to convince others that they're in the presence of departed loved ones. 'When you come into the room, it's not helping me ... It's not easy in this phosphorescent gloom, Telling waking dreams apart anyhow'.

With piano and off-mic vocals in support, there's a wry awareness of the situation as he continues to try and pull the wool over her eyes. The faking of 'cups and saucers crashing in' as if by spirited hands, continues, as with twinkling keyboards 'Houdini applauds the gag again' – an allusion to the fact that most people clap at the wrong times during magic tricks, magicians applauding the seemingly mundane moments when nothing happens, as that is where the trickery is achieved. Within all this fakery, 'No one's a true believer' – the languid piano solo showing that she hasn't been taken in.

'Ballantines' (Mann) (2:21)

The jaunty bar-room piano suggests the *Cheers* theme, but the words are the opposite – no one is glad you came. Their downcast tone tells of one who used to be on top of the world but has lost his position of influence, the pointed digs reminding him how hard it is 'Ringing the bells of doors that don't swing wide anymore' whilst 'Hearing the sound of voices just inside'. Once an insider, he's now shut out, probably on a professional level, the suggestion being that alcohol has been his downfall and he's the architect of his own demise. The use of the name Ballantines most likely refers to the American brewing company. Aimee and Sean Hayes trade lines before coming together to duet:

And men who couldn't hold your coat
Once hung on every anecdote
So it must be hard watching the fellows gloat

His former underlings now jeer at this new position in life. Whatever he has done under the influence, he's unlikely to be forgiven for. The severity of the misdemeanours (which 'could only horrify the elite') will see the 'same old crowd just pass you by in the street'. The bridge (with added trombone from Jason Thor to underscore the frivolity) gives more detail:

The patrons at the bar
In Lexington, Kentucky
Once sprung for every drink you downed
With things the way they are
It's not that kind of party
If what you've got just might be going around

Even his fellow barflies don't want to know him, in case, by doing so, bad luck becomes contagious. Vocal mimics brass in a lighthearted and woozy solo. The singers don't appear overly concerned, and the song's object appears to be getting what he deserves – his fellow 'fat cats' won't be 'getting thin' by stressing about the jam he's now in. There's no value in considering the matter further, he isn't coming back. Aimee and Sean join again to sweetly harmonise that the answer is to get another round in, ending the album in fine form.

Ballantines? Ballantines. Ballantines!

Related Songs
'Lullaby' (Mann) (3:59)

As the title suggests, it's easy-going, a country feel in the slide guitar, including a beautiful solo. But it's mainly driven by acoustic guitar and piano. The tone is melancholy, Aimee's voice warm and comforting as the first verse gives an evocative image of the monotony of life on the road in, 'a fifteen-passenger van ... Tryin' to make everything right'. It's not an easy life, 'No one can keep their demons at bay, At some point, you're gonna give your secrets away' – the singer watching the object of their love from a distance:

> I see what goes on but I don't say a word
> It's none of my business what dreams you've deferred

The chorus delivers the bittersweet 'And you will do just what you always do, Close your eyes and let her run to you, And I know cause I'd run to you too'. In the final verse, the singer opens her heart, although to herself, and it seems he will never know how she feels. 'Baby, I love you, what more do you want? Loves that can't hurt you and ghosts that won't haunt?'. It's a lovely song, a bonus on the album's *iTunes* release.

'At The Edge Of The World' (Mann, Zach Gill) (2:50)

Another from the *Arctic Tale* movie, this one played over the opening credits. Acoustic guitars and piano chime in an icy duet with co-writer Zach Gill, the words describing the endless sea of white where the animal heroes forge a living in the face of global warming. The voices blend beautifully in the chorus, which is wordy but highly evocative:

> At the edge of the world rising out of the snow like a kind of frozen cathedral
> There is mother of pearl lining blankets of ice at the edge of the world
> And no one knows what it's like on the clear blue ocean
> Along the shadows of ice on the deep blue sea

A light but worthy track, and something different for Aimee.

Charmer (2012)

Personnel:
Aimee Mann: Vocals, Acoustic Guitar
James Mercer: Vocals
J.J. Johnson, Jay Bellerose: Drums and Percussion
Chris Bruce: Electric Guitar
Paul Bryan: Bass, Mellotron, Background Vocals
Jebin Bruni: Piano, Keyboards
Jamie Edwards: Electric Guitar, Piano, Keyboards, Tubular Bells
Michael Penn: Background Vocal
Producer: Paul Bryan
Recorded: Stampede Origin (L.A.), Paul Bryan's Home Studio
Record Label: SuperEgo
Released: 17 September 2012
Running Time: 38:02
Highest chart place: US:33, UK:74

Aimee was a guest at the White House in 2011 for the American Poetry Celebration:

It had a really big impact, way bigger than I expected. Don't get me wrong,
I knew it was a big gig. But I also didn't think it would have this big spiritual
impact on me. Hearing the poets talk was really inspiring and honestly made
me think totally differently about the purpose of art, which I think heretofore
I thought was just a nice add-on if everything else is taken care of – like a
fun little frill for life. But I started to realise there's something more essential
about art, and it's kind of the thing that makes the difference from being just a
group, like a herd, to being a civilization.

She appeared on comedy sketch show, *Portlandia*, playing herself working as
a cleaner as she needs a second job to make ends meet. 'That was a true story.
Carrie (Brownstein, one of the show's stars) had hired a cleaning service, and
the girl who showed up was a singer in a band they liked. And yeah, more
people have recognised me from *Portlandia* than music in the last year.'
    As Aimee told *The Daily Record*, 'Quite a while had passed before I woke up
and thought it was probably time for me to put out another record. You cannot
underestimate my inertia.' *Charmer* eventually arrived in 2012. A move away
from the previous record, the guitars were back. This is a power-pop record,
featuring songs about those who charm, and those who fall under their spell,
as discussed in a *Mojo* interview at the time.

I've always been fascinated by people who are charming. Because, in the
best sense of the word, those people are really fun to be around, they drive
the social interaction and it's on a continuum. But from *charming* you can
get to *narcissistic*, and from that you can get *manipulative*, and eventually

sociopath. So for me, it's interesting to see where people fall on that, to see how they can get what they want with their charm.

The title song was the catalyst, but there isn't a full-blown theme: 'There are obviously songs that aren't really on that topic, but it was a thing that I kept coming back to...'.
Rock's Back Pages asked where *she* stood on the charmer scale:

I'm not great ... Where you wanna be sitting, is a person who's present and interested in you, and asks you questions about yourself, and have a modicum of entertainment in your own conversation, and stories that you relate. I don't think I come up to that level. I think I'm more stilted and uncomfortable, and I feel like I could really use some more charm.

Chicago Music Guide **noted that 'The characters Mann writes about tend not to think such noble thoughts, but if art is largely making something functional out of dysfunction, then Mann just might be our laureate ... She's the kind of artist who'd rather disarm than charm, though maybe you'd be forgiven for even applying the C-word to her bracing musical bewitchery.'**
Again produced by Paul Bryan, *Charmer* **takes the feel of the keyboard focused** *@#%&*! Smilers* **and integrates guitars to make an interesting hybrid. The keyboards don't dominate the sound but add integral elements, Aimee sticking to acoustic guitar, with a band featuring a cast of regular collaborators, plus a duet with James Mercer of indie rock band, The Shins.**

This time, I wanted to use more analogue synthesizers, because the music I was inspired by was that real '70s kind of thing. You know on (Blondie's) *Parallel Lines*, when they were first putting synths in, but they were still being played almost like guitars? When I go back and listen to that stuff now, I go, 'Oh, this is basically a rock band with just some *bloopity bloopity* keyboards on top'. I love that. I wanted to go back to 'Remember when synthesizers were super-fun and brand new?'.

There's a particularly natural and organic feel, Aimee confirming that 'most of the record is the band playing live in the studio. Probably two takes', and it comes through beautifully.

We wanted something slightly different, a little poppier. And obviously, some of those sort of new wavey Cars/Split Enz things were an influence. I was thinking classic pop, and what that meant to me. So there was a bit of Jimmy Webb and, you know, a couple of different influences, but a lot of pop.

Regarding her lack of bass playing, she confirmed her deference to Paul Bryan in an interview with *Rock's Back Pages***:**

I can't argue with it. What am I gonna say – 'Um, I think a version of what you are doing but, like, way dumber, and not as proficient, is what's needed'? I'm kind of used to it because then we can track live, and I play acoustic, and I'm more locked-in to the rhythm of the song when I'm singing if I can play acoustic. So I would never be able to play bass live in the studio. I can do it live, but you kind of have to learn how to sing and play the song at the same time – two halves of the brain have to co-ordinate.

Ed Sherman's cover artwork hints at the hypnotic effect that charmers have on those they encounter, the colours and style suggesting consistency with *@#%&*! Smilers* while being completely different. The swirling images compound the unsettling sense, continued into the booklet, where lyrics in adjacent columns are disconcertingly printed upside-down against each other.

Reviews were generally positive, although *Rolling Stone* was critical of the lyrics and production. *Mojo* noted the 'Americana and power-pop ... swaddled in the choicest vintage tones', while *The Independent* called it 'Another sweet viper's bite of post-Freudian dyspepsia from the singer-songwriter who loves to mistrust', and *Q* considered it 'Good and snarky'.

'Charmer' (Mann) (3:25)

Having spent considerable time with musicians, comedians and record industry types, Aimee is intimately familiar with the dealings of charmers. 'They're usually people who you really like being around in the beginning, and then they're very exhausting after a while, because they require an audience. But that's very seductive ... You yourself are complicit in the interaction of the charmer. As soon as you think somebody likes you, then you suddenly think, "What a great guy!".'

The lyric describes the charmer gathering interactions like apples from a tree, with a compulsion to take something from everyone they meet ('quite the little collector'). Their targets respond, as 'They can't see the hidden agenda you got going on'. Mann looks at the charmer's frailties. They 'feel like they're frauds' – the adoration even more alluring when they have to work harder to get it:

> But when you're weak, it's the Holy Grail
> You're two for one, it's a fire sale
> And that's a wall that you cannot scale
> So you're forced to burrow under

There's an element of self-hate for how they are, 'A victim of sideshow hypnosis'. But they can't fight it – 'You only can surrender'.

The genesis of the music came, at least in part, from an unusual source: 'The theme from *The Rockford Files*. It's actually quoted at the end. So that kind of sound, synthesizers when they're used in that way'.

A quirky synth line is the first thing you hear, ahead of the chugging rhythm.

It's slightly cheesy, but it works, and the sound is immediately a blend of the last few albums. A variety of keyboard textures are deployed as lead instruments throughout, adding key phrases and hooks in an upbeat sound. The bass sound is different, more grungy, as she confirmed to *Rock's Back Pages*. 'It's the first time Paul's playing with the pick and turning up the treble. We've had the treble completely off for about a decade!'

Released as a single, the fun video (directed by comedian Tom Scharpling) stars Laura Linney and John Hodgman. While chatting, Hodgman suggests to Aimee that she could deploy a robot double to go on tour and do meet-and-greets in her place. A perfect deal! Except, after being trained to take Mann's place, the android (Linney) proves to be better at it than the star, and has to be terminated. Regarding Linney's involvement, Mann said, 'She's really fantastic. That she would agree to do something like that, for no money and in 100-degree heat... It's unbelievable'.

'Disappeared' (Mann) (3:24)

Regarding someone who is popular, but 'makes a big production out of cutting people off, and in your relationship with them, you always think, "Well, they'll never do that to me"', sung from the perspective of the person who has been *disappeared*. Having wound up on the 'bad' side, they join 'the queue of people dead to you, The one-time chosen few':

> That's all, that's it
> You got yourself disappeared
> The atom split
> And you got back-engineered
> You're a forgotten face
> Behind a beard
> That's it, that's all, you're gone

But, 'Was every enemy, Bad as you made him be? Or were they just some gullible stooge like me?'. Did they deserve the 'Irish goodbye' of a friendship abruptly ending with no further contact?

The first sounds are the *Tommy*-influenced phased synths, guitar taking the mid-tempo lead, with prowling bass. The chorus is appealingly laid-back, with punchy words underlining the lack of care for erased friends. It's very satisfying.

'Labrador' (Mann) (3:49)

The video for this second single unexpectedly recreates the 'Voices Carry' promo that raised Aimee's profile so much in the 1980s. The accompanying behind-the-scenes clip is hysterical, Aimee hamming it up about how devious director Tom Scharpling coerced her into doing it against her wishes. As she told Spinner, it was a case of 'trusting somebody else having an idea and trusting that that idea would come off really well. (Scharpling's) instincts are so dead on, and he felt like there was sort of a nostalgic interest (in recreating it) but also a ridiculousness factor, especially if the setup was that I was coerced into it. He thought (that) was really funny, and I totally agree. I thought it was a real inspired idea'.

In this version, her partner tries to give her a braid like Aimee had in the 1980s, resulting in her standing in the theatre and singing 'Labrador', much to his embarrassment.

The song itself is a strident rocker, with a piano intro, swelling keys, and doubled vocal in the chorus. A piano motif is central, and there's a lovely keyboard solo with a particularly nostalgic air after the bridge – Mellotron accenting the following verse.

The words take in a different sort of charmer – Maisie the family dog, whose loyalty made a deep impression on Aimee as a child ('Remember good old Maisie, How she waited at the stairs for you'). But here the protagonist is likened to the dog, in thrall to someone who shouldn't do what they do, but is incapable of changing. 'You lie so well, I could never even tell, What were facts in your artful rearranging'. The tone of the music is so light that the darkness in the words is easy to miss. It's about control and loyalty in the face of adversity, the 'Voices Carry' referencing working very well. The chorus focuses the issue:

But I came back for more
And you laughed in my face and you rubbed it in
'Cause I'm a Labrador
And I run when the gun drops the dove again

Looking back to the early days, they were 'glad to be your pet', doing as they were told. But 'You got bored, You got mad, Then you got crazy'. As the relationship continued, she would always 'come back for more', stressing that she's okay with the controlling situation – 'Believe me, my dear, I'm not complaining' – but do we believe it? It sounds like a cry for help, and the video implies a final breaking-free.

'Crazytown' (Mann) (3:21)
This one revolves around 'one of my favourite topics, the crazy girlfriend'.

I have a friend who goes out with these girls who always wear short, tight dresses and high heels. They all refer to themselves as *spontaneous*, which to me is code for 'I'm crazy, and if we're driving down the street, I might just hang out the window and yell at passers-by'. Or if someone describes themselves as *passionate*, I honestly think that's a code word for 'I will make scenes and throw shit at you in public places'.

Mann described the alcoholic young woman protagonist to *The Daily Telegraph* as, 'a manic pixie dream girl. She seems up for anything, running down the street barefoot. But next thing you know, she's throwing up in your car. There's a certain type of guy who goes for that girl – the caretaker, who's very present and sober. And these people go together. The crazy girl can't flourish without the fixer'.

'Crazytown' is more 'about a relationship, but it could also be about a friendship, or about a guy taking care of his alcoholic mother. You know, it is very sad to have friends who are crazy and can't take care of themselves. And you can't get too far into it, because then you'll be dwelling in the world of crazy, and there's no getting out'.

From 'Another girl who threatens suicide, You called the cops, But then she denied every word', the scene changes:

> And you know you'll be the one who's paying the tab for her
> You're out there trying to flag a cab

And for who? A girl from Crazytown, 'Where craziness gets handed down', and if you volunteer to be part of her world, that's where you'll be living too. His vision of the girl is a dream of someone who doesn't exist – 'And she enlisted a fool'. It was fun to start with, 'But now, son, you'll be posting bond', and you can't seem to get out of it. The CD booklet gives a stark warning: 'Good Luck'.

A piano drone and synth hook lead into a swinging verse with a 1950s feel, the chorus bursting out, a thing of beauty with a rough guitar edge. The bridge and the lead into the final chorus add a different flavour, in a classy arrangement that takes in many facets of Aimee's sound. A dreaminess and lightness of touch carry a gritty message, which the hook delivers with precision. Pop the way it should be done.

'Soon Enough' (Mann, Tim Heidecker) (3:59)

The third single is one of several tracks here inspired by TV shows – this one: *Intervention*.

> Another show I watch religiously! Everybody's reading their letters and everybody's crying, while once again, the target of the intervention is like, 'Fuck all y'all!'. It's so classic. So the narrator of the song is like, 'Yeah, I know, we're all a bunch of assholes, we're all against you. Just sit and listen to the letters, and soon enough you can say what a bunch of jerks we are. We get it.'

Of comedian and co-writer Tim Heidecker, Aimee told *Penny Black* '(He) has a great musical sense, you know? He writes a lot of songs. He has an idea; it's usually a parody song, usually an anti-Trump song. He writes fast, he records it and it comes out later that afternoon, which is something I can't manage, but I think he's got a real good melodic sense'.

The video is a filmed intervention, Aimee surprised by friends and relatives. Show host Heidecker leads, his flip chart showing phrases like 'I miss the old

Aimee!'. A cake is presented featuring her image saying 'I'm sorry, I'll get help'. The host annoys everyone until Aimee leaves, the closing image confirming that '6 months later, Aimee is doing great', accompanied by her face on a half-eaten slice of cake.

Spacey 1950s sci-fi synth, leads in – guitar, bass, drums and piano taking the strain. The words describe the intervention. 'Everybody's got their secrets out, So sad, Go around the room and see who doesn't cry'. Soon enough, it'll be time to move on, but:

> You can say we made it up
> Just for fun I guess
> To make a mess
> Cause what's more fun
> Than other people's hell?

There's a warning to 'kill the whole vindictive bit, 'Cause you'll someday realize there's ties you'll want to use' – the chorus lifting things effortlessly on a strong hook with supporting Beatle-esque vocals. The variations work well, with Jamie Edwards' sinuous and engaging guitar solo. It's sparky, engaging, and smoothly delivered with keen attention to detail.

'Living A Lie' (Mann, Paul Bryan) (3:26)
This resulted from another planned stage musical. When Aimee met Aaron Sorkin (writer of *West Wing* and *The Social Network*), he told her about an idea he had.

> Obviously he's got 50 million projects, so I don't know if it's something that'll ever happen. But he told me the basic plot of it, and just as an exercise, I thought, 'Suppose this is the song these two characters sing where their relationship is really falling apart'. It makes me laugh, because two people singing a duet is usually a love song, and these are two people that are ripping each other to shreds. 'You narcissist!' 'Oh yeah? Well, you're this has-been who thinks he's so great.' I should write a whole record of vicious duets.

Lead vocals are shared with James Mercer. 'Because it's such a duet-y duet, we wanted to get somebody who really had a great voice, and we were just lucky that he was game.'

After the synth and guitar intro, it's a straight-ahead rock song with edgy keyboard additions. It's all about the voices, which alternate between verses, joining together for the chorus. James' sneering first verse mocks her vanity and social-climbing ways. She retorts spikily, calling him 'A boy genius, Just past his prime' – living in a golden cage and waiting for 'People to blame, Bridges to burn'. The chorus confirms that they both know that they're living the same lie, waiting for the shell of togetherness to finally crack.

The extended bridge is split to great effect. In a slightly pared-down setting, he remembers their first meeting and how she created a mythology about herself to impress him. Aimee comes in beautifully and warmly, to point out his narcissism and how he gloats at the bowing and scraping of underlings – all ending in a swirl of synths. They are not going to resolve this.

'Slip And Roll' (Mann) (4:12)

Aimee sings to someone who is always hiding, coming out fighting when confronted. They seem larger than life – 'So charming that it was disarming' – but there's an insecurity, and she wonders about the reality behind the façade. The title's defensive boxing move is carried into the chorus. 'Stick the jab, kid, Don't just trade the punches ... Slip and roll till you're ready to take the hit'. He dodges the perceived attacks, but he isn't really listening. The glorious bridge is the centrepiece:

> And you can take it, take it, take it, take it
> We've all seen that guy take it on the chin
> Oh, take it, take it, I know you can take it
> But when will you take something in

World-weary, it's slow and relaxed, in many ways akin to *The Forgotten Arm*. The guitar carries an easy western drawl, warming into the chorus with its skilfully delivered hook, Chris Bruce's solo underscoring the country feel.

'Gumby' (Mann) (2:53)

Aimee explained the inspiration here as coming from an episode of US reality show, *Hoarders* – a man's compulsion rendering his daughter homeless.

> The thing I was fascinated by is that you have people who are desperate to help their loved ones who are living in squalor, and often in dangerous circumstances, but the hoarders themselves do nothing but resent the help. They just see that you're trying to take their shit from them, and they constantly position themselves to be the victim of these people who are coming in trying to help. It's really delusional.

The unusual title has nothing to do with *Monty Python*, or the claymation character. Aimee just thought it was a good name for a hoarder!

It's a toe-tapper, the sunny and jovial upbeat swing masking the sadness of the chorus, which almost pleads with the hoarder to call their daughter. Frustration seeps through in the verses. Fear of change is at its heart: 'Why move? Moving is how things begin'. But the place is a mess:

> The front yard taken by the crows
> Black guards with their shiny pieces of tin
> So much fury you bury it in

Things are getting harder
And getting more out of hand

All those trinkets bought and sold
All tokens you've thrown down to the abyss
There's a bottom that you'll never hit

She tries the direct approach with, 'Dude, you're not even that old'.

And I don't know just how you explain this
To a kid with nowhere to live
Tell her that the father she has means well
But just has nothing to give

The chorus features lovely backing, and it's a heartfelt plea for someone to turn their life around for the benefit of those dear to them.

'Gamma Ray' (Mann) (3:00)

The protagonist is likened to the electromagnetic radiation of the title, the cell-killing most-energetic form of light. This person lives for thrills, and is a danger to others, dragging them down. But life will generally find a way: 'You can't keep everyone at bay'.

It's a sparse lyric with a basic chorus, the problem starting with 'a great big bang'. 'One thing leads to another and none of it's good'. There's frustration in 'And guess who's gonna have to play the jailer?, And guess who's gonna lead the chain gang?'. It's all about fostering flaws and not forgiving weakness. 'From that you've been turned into a monster, A nightmare that you force yourself to live'.

The album's hardest-rocking track, the clattering percussion and guitar shards give momentum. It's as direct as Aimee gets, a rumbustious kick-ass song – like the flashing of a radiation warning, with a hint of sirens in the distant synth part.

'Barfly' (Mann) (4:00)

Written previously and revisited for *Charmer*.

This kind of thing happens all the time, where you get asked to write a song for something. Someone gives you a documentary about the time Jack Kerouac was trying to dry out in Big Sur in Northern California, so I thought 'Great', and I wrote this song. And then I don't really know what happened. I think the movie came out, but my song didn't get included. So I finished it up.

From the opening slinky guitar riff, you can feel the dereliction in the laid-back shuffle and 'Spent my nights in a sleeping bag smelling kerosene, Thinking fog and sand was gonna keep me clean'. The strong two-part chorus is a rising call to the barfly. 'You won't get high, You'll just get down ... So do the time'. The blurring cadence reflects the drunken scenario, with a vivid augmented-reality:

Took a breath full of iodine and I overdosed
And the tide crept high
Like a watery ghost
And no one needs your kind
Of a dope-sick clown
You can always find
Sitting one seat down

The tone of sympathy in 'I can't see how, You deserve all the mess that even guilt won't allow' is followed by Chris Bruce's confident guitar solo, supported by Mellotron, and tinged with sadness, ending on a wall of synth drone.

'Red Flag Diver' (Mann) (2:29)

Short and sweet (or as Aimee noted, 'Short, creepy and sweet!'), taking in a scuba diving scene, the red flag a warning to other vessels that a diver is below. It is indeed sweet-sounding, jangly acoustic set against a melodic lead line. A siren draws the hapless 'diver' down, overpowered by her charms, to a place where 'You'll be miserable, But I'll be free', topping it off with a mysterious 'I'm as good for you as I can be'. The bridge discloses the controlling nature of the potential relationship:

Cause first I'll want it
And then I won't want it
And then I'll just scuttle it all
On rocks where sirens call

Keyboard lines and percussion, rise and fall like the whitecap waves. It's a lovely way to end, relaxing as it washes over you with Aimee's warm and inviting voice. But heed the warnings and stay away – danger lurks beneath.

Related Tracks
'Brother's Keeper' (Mann, Paul Bryan) (4:01)

A 7" bonus single with pre-orders of the vinyl album at some US record stores, this song appeared on the Australian and Japanese versions of *Charmer*. A splash of drums and a fanfare of keys, and we're off on a solid rhythm with piano supporting the vocal. There's a fairground freak show element to 'Come see your Jane try to train every devil in her, There's not a man alive who could tame this creature, You better leave the professor behind, see what time will teach her' – the second verse adding 'Shit's just a trick and each week's full of compromises, She'll push for a fish like a seal clapping for its prizes'.

Paul Bryan supports the vocal in the pre-chorus as we 'get a little glimpse of the disaster to come'. The chorus itself is an upbeat and engaging sing-along, as we leave the hapless subject to his own devices. 'You're not your brother's keeper, now, Your brother's on his own, That's how the seeds of avarice are sown'. There's a lovely tone and a beautiful arrangement, the bridge changing the pace on a variety of keyboard textures, before launching into the final chorus variation:

> And after the fail, you can wail as they drag the lever
> Silence the band, wring the hand that you didn't give her
> And every man alive has to sign a waiver
> To put a coin in the plate so that fate won't return the favour

With the payoff, 'Tell them dust is dust and men are men, And men all act alone', this is a great song.

'Mea Culpa' (Mann) (2:27)

Flip side of the 'Brother's Keeper' 7" (and also on the Australian album). Voice and acoustic guitar, along with the tone of the words, give it a folk feel, Aimee offering a lilting sadness. Sombre keys from Jebin Bruni join in the second round to give an orchestral edge, and there's stark and melodic beauty. The title acknowledges one's own fault, giving clues to the meaning. There's confessional language in 'Trinity Church', 'What's one penitent more?', 'That's how you atone' and 'Bless me, Father'. But there are also nautical themes, with the Liberty Bell 'affixed to the prow' and 'Neptune's watery hell lives inside of you now', as the male focus grimly washes ashore. Is she confessing her infidelities ('Let her shoot, Let her have her massacre, Blood dripping down in the snow')? Despite him being able to 'tell her everything ... She never wanted to know', and ultimately she seems guilty about the way he has been treated and the damage she has caused. Another beautiful song, too good for the *Rarities* tag.

'Salvation' (Mann) (3:46)

There's a stalking quality, with bass and acoustic guitar to start, electric joining in, the fast-paced verse evocative and interesting:

> The carbon on the fingerprint
> That's lifted from the lighter's flint
> That caused another smoker's squint
> Who sees the point but not the light
>
> And rabble-rousing diatribes
> Revealing more for what it hides
> Who plays a little off the sides

Who swears they can sin in spite
Of salvation

Aimee sings the chorus in her higher registers with piano accompaniment, and there's a sweeping instrumental end-section. Another fine song.

But everywhere is two-way glass
And double locks and easy pass
Turn oxygen to laughing gas

So I laughed until I cried
Then I chose another side
When you asked me to decide
Between you and staying alive

'I'm Cured' (Lyrics: Mann, Stephen Levinson, Rob Kutner, Joel Moss Levinson; Music: Mann, Joel Moss Levinson) (2:52)
Recorded in 2014 to support *OneKid OneWorld*, a charity targeting projects to benefit children in need. This acoustic number, with piano and accordion from Joel Levinson, describes the heartache and sense of loss felt by a common-cold germ when a cure is finally found. The video features Aimee as the germ in blue bodysuit and furry headgear, as lab scientists beaver away. 'I'm cured, but not from you' she sings, kissing a scientist before sneezing. It's a fun video, briefly featuring comedy actor, Fred Melamed, the song included on the *OneKid OneWorld* project's *2776* album.

The Both (2014)

Personnel:
Aimee Mann: Vocals, Bass, Acoustic Guitar
Ted Leo: Vocals, Electric Guitar
Paul Bryan: Acoustic and Electric Guitars, Bass, Piano, Mellotron, Chamberlin,
Backing Vocals
Scott Seiver: Drums and Percussion
Producer: Paul Bryan
Record Label: SuperEgo
Recorded: Stampede Origin
Released: 15 April 2014
Running Time: 41:59
Highest chart place: US:59, UK:-

In April 2013, Mann appeared on *The Daily Show,* in a mock appeal to
unexpectedly preserve the habitat of the crab louse, in a comedy segment
about pubic shaving! That July, she filed a lawsuit against MediaNet Digital for
distributing her songs on an expired license agreement, later settling out of
court.

Another solo album would be a while off. After the *Charmer* tour, she went
straight into working with singer and guitarist, Ted Leo, after they became
friends when he played support on the tour. She told *Consequence of Sound*:

> There was really no break between any of that. It was kind of like a four-year
> period from the fall of 2012 on, four solid years of just going and going and
> going. I suddenly just sort of collapsed right after finishing this record. I was
> like, 'Man, I can't imagine going on tour right now', or doing anything for that
> matter.

She found working with Ted inspirational. 'He makes a live show really fun.
So that made me really want to be in a band with him. That was a very specific
feeling, just playing on stage. I wanted to do more of that. I really liked his
songwriting, I liked him as a performer. He's an incredible musician.' She
noted that collaborating in such a way 'takes the pressure off. The most fun
thing about being a musician, is being part of a unit that works together, where
you can hear that a totally different thing springs up. That is definitely more
satisfying to me personally than being out there all on your own. Sometimes
it's lonely by yourself'.

For the first time in 25 years, Aimee found herself in a band, initially styled
as #BOTH, later becoming The Both. Writing began in December 2012, vocals
shared on the recordings, with Mann returning to playing bass regularly. She
told *Stereogum* 'I like playing in a rock band, and if it's louder, I like to be the
bass player.' An EP was initially planned, but Leo felt they were just getting
started, and an album was completed instead.

By taking 'stems of an idea and kick(ing) them back and forth', the long-distance writing process ended up with 'songs where each person has their verse, the chorus may be written by one person, the bridge written by the other. But there are definitely songs where we would go over line-by-line or just ask each other questions' to 'focus the narrative'.

The sound is rocky and stripped-down, influenced by Leo's grounding in punk, with pop leanings. The live shows featured a power trio set up with drummer Scott Seiver, Aimee enjoying the diversion. On the band's website, she said 'Honestly, I feel like for the first time I'm part of a rock band. I guess it really is just the two of us, but I think of it as a band, you know, like the Captain & Tennille were a band.'

Humour was never far away, as seen in the promo videos – the shared sense of fun and friendship helping to focus their individual skills on a joint love of harmony and melody. Leo noted that 'It's still revealing itself, to a certain degree. Because we are constantly meshing and pulling apart and coming together over the course of songs, or even just individual lines in songs, I'm discovering more than ever things I'd never even thought about that appeal to me'. He confirmed learning a lot from Aimee's exacting way with words, helping him to 'get over any ego issues with the editing and collaborative writing because it really is fun to sit down with her and tinker and treat it like a puzzle'.

The album reflects the feel of the live shows, Seiver's drums driving the songs along, producer Paul Bryan adding acoustic guitar and occasional keyboard parts that point towards Aimee's sound. But it's Aimee, Ted, and their songs, in the spotlight, together with an unexpected Thin Lizzy cover. Regarding the rocky edge and the contrasts in their individual styles, Aimee noted to Leo that 'Anything you sing on, you have an energy to your singing that declares it a rock song. And I have this fucking sleepy Karen Carpenter thing to voice that's absolutely not in my control, that declares it to be a folk song, and that's just how it is. I could sing a song that's super-fast with constant drum fills and solos, and it would still lilt'.

Ed Sherman's artwork features Ted and Aimee in Ken and Barbie form, cutting letters out of their ghost logo to spell out the band name. There are also cutouts of the pair, with clothes and instruments to dress them in!

The Both is an unexpected and pivotal late-period album in Aimee's career, packed with energy and a collaborative dynamic that shows both principles to their best advantage. It seems to have brought the fun back for Aimee, and it's an excellent album in its own right. In 2017, Aimee noted to *The Observer* that they would certainly do another record, although nothing has appeared to date other than the duo's 2019 podcast series *The Art of Process*.

'The Gambler' (Mann, Leo) (3:08)

While the other songs were written from a blank slate, this one was around before The Both. Ted played it while supporting Mann, who said, 'Every time

I heard it, I kept having this urge to play bass on it and sing on it, and I'm not a person who jumps on stage and wants to jam with other people – it's not my thing!'. Ted confirmed that he wrote the song with Aimee in mind and was very happy that she wanted to do it. 'It was the intersection of where we were musically, it's like kind of encapsulated in that song.'

A power trio opening, Ted takes the first verse, Aimee joining for the last line and into the second. Ted adds a few solo lines before singing the first stripped-down part of the bridge, Aimee coming in for the second half. It's a strong opener, and it's nice to hear Aimee in this setting.

Lyrically, having ignored the warnings, he wakes to find that things have gone awry. 'I hear you unlock my door, I don't want you to have my key anymore ... The well's dry, I'm out of empathy'. He's invested in the relationship but has nothing to show for it.

> This shouldn't end with both of us dead
> I'd like to help you
> But we've been here before
> Yes, I'm aware of the stakes
> I can't afford any more

It ends with the finality of 'You're a gambler in need, and I want you to go'.

'Milwaukee' (Mann, Leo) (4:21)

Talking to *Rolling Stone*, Leo remembered walking along Milwaukee's riverfront before a show in 2012, and being 'startled by a very disconcerting bronze statue of Arthur Fonzarelli, aka "The Fonz", aka "The Bronze Fonz". In that very moment, we knew we had to start a band to immortalise it (more than a bronze statue already immortalises something), and The Both was born'.

It's a kick-ass rocker with a conversational tone, Aimee taking the first verse, remembering the statue, Leo picking it up to describe the show. The duet chorus is a roof-raising ear-worm with fine soloing from Leo, gradually slowing to an elegant finish.

In the video, Ted and Aimee need a drummer at short notice. Ted's uncle 'Ed' Leo (played by Ted) is available, and Aimee is willing to give it a go. But things don't go to plan.

An exclusive special edition of the album was available through Barnes & Noble, featuring an acoustic version of this song.

'No Sir' (Mann, Leo) (3:46)

The echoing guitar intro makes this edgier, and a nice contrast. Aimee sings the first two verses, the second with lovely Mellotron accompaniment. There's 'a shadow in the wings ... You can hear it in his voice, But you don't have a choice, No sir'. In the chorus, Leo takes the high harmony, switching roles for the second half, as their voices blend well.

Work on your story, Sir
Are you worried her mood's gonna waver and change?
Don't blame the world or the girl
For what keeps you estranged

The guitar tone is rough and punky, while Mann's bass is full and to the fore. Leo takes the final verse, the outcome seeming brighter. It's a difficult upstream journey, 'But you won't make it there alone'. Again, an acoustic version appeared as a bonus on the special edition.

'Volunteers of America' (Mann, Leo) (3:44)

The second single is a summery sing-along, opaque words not giving much away. They seem to discuss the position of the US as *the world's policeman*. 'When you see smoke, You run toward the fire 'cause you must', but you then have to pick up the consequences. Later verses take a pop at religion – 'just because, You're mad at the cross on the wall', that 'hole in your side', 'Where bodies aren't bodies, They're bread' – so I suspect there's an element of despair with right-wing traditionalism.

There's an ironic reference to the inscription on the Statue of Liberty in:

So bring out your poor
Your washed on the shore
Your refuse, your teeming depressed
You take them all in
'Cause that's where you've been
A person who has to say 'yes'

The bass has a treated texture, the verses again split between the singers, with shared choruses. It's another rollicking stomp-along, with a highly defined melody, the frantic roughness of the guitar solo working well, with acoustic guitar filling out the sound.

The video features an outdoor wedding celebration, Susannah Hoffs of The Bangles featuring in the wedding band, guests Ted and Aimee called up to perform the song with them. Uncle 'Ed' Leo also appears, but his drumming services are, on this occasion, not required. Interestingly, the marrying couple is veteran actor Russ Tamblyn and his wife Bonnie.

'Pay for It' (Mann, Leo) (3:16)

This one jumps straight into the chorus with a repeated 'You're gonna make me wait for it, You're gonna make me pay for it now', the verse split, lines sung individually with some in harmony, supported by lyrical guitar figures. There's a slinky feel and a nice groove, Ted soloing darkly before the lovely bridge with its 1960s horn section vibe in the keyboard line.

The words look at two sides of a relationship. To start, she seems happy and 'never alone', but the domestic idyll doesn't seem enough for him. When he says he's had enough, she suggests he moves in with a friend, which she doesn't expect him to follow through on – the vindictive nature of the chorus coming into play as everything falls apart.

It's a toe-tapper, but perhaps overburdened by the extended and repetitive chorus.

'You Can't Help Me Now' (Mann, Leo) (3:39)

This starts in more regular Aimee territory, an acoustic intro and a gentle pace. She sings sweetly, supported by Leo's guitar. The duet chorus is simple but effective, the contrast with Leo singing the second verse, nicely established. Paul Bryan plays bass here, the bridge again benefiting from keyboard additions, as Aimee sings high.

This was the first song written jointly, started by Leo who remembers being shaken when he received Mann's initial notes. She told *The Boston Globe*, 'A person who I respect so much is handing me negative notes about something I wrote. It was really just my own quaking ego. But we got past that pretty quickly.' Leo described the partnership with Mann as 'The best thing that has happened to my writing process in my life'.

The first verse has Mann's hand all over it:

Anytime you establish a world of your own, you get thrown
Try and answer a bomb with a calm undertone, alone
I wanted you to know that I put up a fight
But everything goes missing when they dim the light
The catastrophic sinking of the windless kite

Set against the resignation of 'And even you can't help me now' in the chorus, the situation is bad, but you have to do what you need to for yourself to make it better. Look forward, don't focus on the past as 'Those "If only's" only clothe the good in front of you with regret'. It's a hopeful song of better things ahead, but changes have to be made.

'The Prisoner' (Mann, Leo) (4:41)

Crashing in like a metal track, it settles into Leo's first verse. The second has a lovely harmony from Aimee, and the chorus is pure power pop – a sweet hook with buzz saw guitars. Ted's solo is more laid-back than expected, adding a melancholy introspection before the chorus reprise. Aimee sings the bridge before a lovely variation on the first part of the chorus to close. Another class song, presented in a different way that gives the album another facet.

There's a Dutch feel to the first verse, with bicycles, canals and Frysk Hynder ('Frisian Horse', a brand of limited production single malt whisky), to give 'doves communion with the hawks', which leads into 'under wing of the White Owl' (referring to the American cigar brand?).

136

'Following the footprints where the new snow fell' to 'the bones we buried in the yard last season':

I was the one who read the map of stars
The little dipper from the handlebars
But you're the one who saw the bridge
And knew that it was ours

The chorus takes us to the Zuiderzee, as 'The snow in the street is turning gray, All the birds at our feet have flown away, It's complicity and heat on holiday'. But you're a prisoner and have to remain, the song ending on a perhaps more hopeful note as a choice has been made: 'But I'm gonna stay.'

'Hummingbird' (Mann, Leo) (4:04)

Things are tranquil in the forest. Aimee sits by the fire with acoustic guitar, watching a deer wander by. But the hummingbird has sent a message.

He told me they're marching on Monsanto
But the same monolithic structures rise

The pace is easy, with a simple rhythm, guitar adding a glowering presence in the distance. With Mellotron string textures, Ted hits the echo for sinister chiming guitar interjections. In the second verse, he sings of bees ignoring the sirens, the hummingbird continuing his warning.

They're marching on the Capitol
With wings at their back
And fear in their eyes

This song of environmental fragmentation is a very different beast to the rest of the album. Ted delivers the next section in measured tones. 'On the tarmac rows of pirouetting jets wait gravely in their lanes, While from our windows, Getting higher we see hybrids wandering the plains'. Sadly, the message seems to have arrived too late and the monolithic structures continue to rise.

'Honesty Is No Excuse' (Phil Lynott) (3:28)

An important catalyst for the project was this cover of Phil Lynott's venerable song from Thin Lizzy's 1971 debut. Ted remembers Aimee hearing it for the first time:

Early Thin Lizzy is not 'The Boys are Back in Town'. It's a lot spookier and more atmospheric and strange. And talking about that particular song is what led to us, I think, really figuring out where a lot of our musical overlap lays. The narrative of the lyrics almost goes maudlin, but it stays on the sharp side

137

of picking apart a personal history of addiction and human failure, and all those things we like to sing about, and I think all that appealed to Aimee.

Ted was holding back during recording, and it was drummer Scott Siever who said 'I don't want to hear what you think you're supposed to do on this record. I want to hear you', and that was when the song took off.

The echoed guitar from the end of 'Hummingbird' bleeds into the start. Aimee takes the first verse, Leo the second, both delivering their lines with passion. Leo pulls out all the stops to reinterpret Eric Bell's original guitar solo. They drop the third and fourth verses and skip through to the last, accompanied by handclaps. Mellotron adds the atmospheric feel of the Lizzy version. It's a cover that fully delivers, and an excellent choice that has hopefully opened up early Thin Lizzy for some.

Lynott's words, even at this early stage of his career, are filled with regret for a life misspent – drinking too much, 'No God, air, water or sunshine', using love offered by others. But at least he has been honest about it, and that's the only excuse he has. You can still hear Lynott's voice singing the words of the second verse: 'A useless rage, a torn-out page, a worn-out gauge, A dirty shade, a big charade, a has-been made', with some redemption in the final verse.

'Bedtime Stories' (Mann, Leo) (4:05)

Scott Miller, founder of power pop bands Game Theory and The Loud Family, was a mutual friend of both Aimee and Ted. Talking to *Pulse!*, Aimee cited The Loud Family's *Plants & Birds & Rocks & Things* as a favourite, noting Miller as 'the best songwriter out there right now, and that was one of my criteria: "Would Scott think that this song is any good?"'. Miller had been pivotal in introducing Aimee and Ted to each other's work, and they intended to meet up while on tour to thank him. But, tragically, he took his own life in April 2013. 'As with any time someone you know dies, you're filled with self-recrimination, and it was just very upsetting', Aimee said. They wrote this song both about Miller and as a tribute, Aimee noting the chorus chord progression as 'very, very Loud Family'.

There's a burst of power pop energy as she delivers the first verse:

Bedtime stories just got the hook
Allegories that stay in the book
So much was simply over
In the little bit of time it took

The vocal harmonies are on the money as Seiver keeps the tempo moving. It's excellent guitar pop, with an underlying sense of sadness, toe-tapping and catchy, sporadic keyboard additions serving the song well.

'The Inevitable Shove' (Mann, Leo) (3:50)

An unusual stomper to end the album in fine form. As always, the short verses are shared, and the chorus a duet, in a song of misdirected recriminations. And it's a *big* chorus: 'You can't blame the ones that you love, But you're still going to blame the ones that you love ... I'm steeling myself for the inevitable shove'. The harmonies are excellent, deft piano lines building a frisky hand-clapping rhythm that keeps things going to the end.

Related Tracks
'Nothing Left To Do (Let's Make This Christmas Blue)' (Mann, Leo) (4:55)
Released in 2014 to support the first of several annual shows curated by Aimee and Ted. *Stereogum* described it as 'A sweet song with some dark lyrics lamenting the feeling of listlessness that can come along with the holiday season'. Aimee clearly has a liking for Christmas songs, and this would have been a good fit on *One More Drifter in the Snow*. She croons the first verse with her customary warmth, Ted joining for the chorus. A traditional Christmas shines through, but the sadness that the season often uncovers is also present. 'Nothing to do but turn the radio on and find a song to listen to ... Tis the season of song and every one reminds me of you'. It gets slightly rockier towards the end, and it's a tasteful and beautiful addition to the Christmas playlist.

'You're a Gift' (Mann, Leo) (3:36)
Aimee and Ted's Christmas song for 2015. It's less traditional than the previous one, barely a Christmas song at all, but sleigh bells will make *any*thing Christmassy! Ironically upbeat, it delivers a wistful air of anxiety and 'longing for someone to hunker down with and enjoy the holiday spirit'. Light, easy and well-performed, a greater sense of urgency arrives with the chorus.

'Independent Together' (Ted Leo, Rebecca Sugar, Stemage) (3:16)
With Aimee having voiced the character, Opal, in the animated TV show *Steven Universe*, Aimee and Ted now sang with Deedee Magno Hall in 2019's movie version. Ted starts quietly, joined by Deedee before the hooky chorus. Aimee joins in after the bridge, and it's a light bit of upbeat optimism.

Mental Illness (2017)

Personnel:
Aimee Mann: Vocals, Bass, Acoustic Guitar, Percussion
Ted Leo: Background Vocals
Paul Bryan: Bass, Background Vocals, String Arrangements and Conducting
Jonathan Coulton: Finger-picked Acoustic Guitar, Background Vocals
Jay Bellerose: Drums and Percussion
Jamie Edwards: Piano, Harmonium, Acoustic and 12-string Guitar
Eric Gorfain, Marisa Kuney, Amy Wickman, Gina Kronstadt, Terry Glenny, Radu Piepta, Susan Chatman: Violin
Leah Katz, Aaron Oltman, Rodney Wirtz: Viola
Richard Dodd, John Krovoza, Peggy Baldwin: Cello
Producer: Paul Bryan
Record Label: SuperEgo
Recorded: Mayberry PCH, United Recordings (L.A.)
Released: 31 March 2017
Running Time: 38:29
Highest chart place: US:54, UK:53

In 2016, Mann appeared on the *@midnight* show with singer-songwriter Jonathan Coulton. He would collaborate on her next solo album, which she started writing after coming off the road with Ted Leo. In response to the rock of *The Both*, 'I was really in the mood to make a record that was as quiet and stripped down and bare-bones as I could possibly manage'. She gave herself a regime of sitting down daily to write.

> I set a timer for fifteen minutes, because I think it gets daunting if you think, 'I have to write a record'. So, I made the task just to sit for fifteen minutes and noodle around on guitar or listen to work tapes or make lists of things, or whatever. Just for fifteen minutes and that was it. If that mushroomed into working on a song and I wanted to keep going, of course I would. But I think that for me, that's how small the task has to be for it to not feel overwhelming. Even the idea of thinking 'It's probably time to start making a new record' can start to seem like pressure, so it's just a way to avoid that. I did have to kind of set a little bit of a goal, just to make sure that I ended up with a guitar in my hand at some point during the day. It's just really easy to have the day get away from you, or get involved in other things.

What appeared were 'softer, melancholy songs,' she told *Stereogum*, 'which is the thing that comes easiest and is most fun for me. It's not a deliberate thing. It's more like "Do what you feel like doing". For other records, I try to make an effort to write a slightly different way, or I make an effort to have more up-tempo songs and more rock songs, so that becomes a little bit more deliberate'.

While touring with Leo, they listened to a lot of Bread on long drives. 'All this super-soft stuff started coming up. It was funny to me, but also charming. The first time around, when I was a kid listening to that music, I thought it was twee: too soft, not cool. Listening to it today, I realise the incredible musicianship and I love how those records sound. So that stuff did become an influence on this record.'

The album was finally completed in the summer of 2016, but she chose not to release it immediately. Having worked solidly since 2012, she took some time off before announcing *Mental Illness* in January 2017. After the 'solid, punchy pop-rock' of *Charmer*, Mann described *Mental Illness* as her 'saddest, slowest and most acoustic, if-they're-all-waltzes-so-be-it record' to date. Indeed, it's an intimate set of predominantly stripped-back acoustic songs, with strings and simple percussion. However, there are more strings than originally intended. Paul Bryan kept producing arrangements that Aimee liked, so the finished record included more strings.

The title was suggested by a friend as a joke, as she told *Penny Black*:

He said, 'What are the songs about?'. I was kind of flippant and said, 'Ah you know, my usual songs about mental illness', and he was like, 'Oh, well you should call it *Mental Illness* then'. And because it's so arresting and so bold, there was something appealing about it, so it kind of stuck with me.

Michael Hausman had pushed for more up-tempo music, but she resisted. It was a conscious decision to make an intimate and acoustic album.

This is really, I think, the most me, because I guess on some level, I come from a fairly folky, 70's singer-songwriter background and I really like that played-on-acoustic-guitar kind of thing. I like to keep it really simple. I like the challenge of having it be interesting even though it is really simple – to use the instrumentation as sparsely as possible. I just feel like you can hear everything, even if what you're hearing is an acoustic guitar. If that's the only instrument you're hearing, you can hear the fingers on the strings and a little bit of string noise and the resonance of the wood and everything. There's something that's just very exciting to me about that. Emotional honesty is uplifting, and it doesn't really matter what the emotion is. It's just uplifting, so that's how I approach it. Writing these songs is never depressing for me, and I don't think you can write out of a position of depression anyway.

Reviews noted the album as sad, folky, intimate and reflective. *The Chicago Tribune* called it Mann's 'sparest, quietest album and also among her most beautiful'.

When asked about the strange amalgam of dark and cute featured in Andrea Desző's cover artwork, Aimee said:

(It) felt like that cover got at the psychological world of that subconscious stuff that's all dark and murky, but there's this creature, and it's kind of a monster, but it's also sort of cute and funny. That's the kind of the attitude I have about having issues and writing songs about your issues and writing songs about other people's issues – that it is dark and difficult and it's a little scary, but also there's an element of humour about it. You know, we're all struggling with the same kinds of things, and there's definitely an element of humour in recognising one of your crazy things in other people or vice versa.

Mann toured the album with a band featuring Jonathan Coulton, who also acted as support. Despite the acoustic setting, it was still expensive to take on the road. She told *Stereogum*, 'There's a lot of manoeuvring to try to keep it viable enough to pay for itself. I couldn't live on what I make touring. As somebody in her fifties, I'm not sleeping on a stranger's couch. It's just too much for me.'

Mental Illness won her another Grammy, for Best Folk Album.

'Goose Snow Cone' (Mann) (3:35)

The pared-down nature of *Mental Illness* shines through on this first single. Tinkling bells set the scene, the main feature being the picked guitar line over which Aimee sings, harmonised beautifully in the chorus. A sliding bass gives a dynamic edge, while the subtle use of the string quartet is simply gorgeous, opening out and embellishing a top-drawer arrangement that makes this fairly simple song fly, fading to nothing on a long bass note to finish.

A song of homesickness, it was started on tour, on a snowy day in Ireland. Aimee saw an Instagram picture of her friend's cat, Goose, her white fur looking like 'a little snowball'. The song developed from this image, drawing in the snowy scene, bells and gentle guitar describing the loneliness she felt at the time. The title was meant to be temporary, 'But I couldn't think of anything I liked better. It's very dumb. But once I wrote the song, I was stuck with it'.

Goose herself took a starring role in the sweet little video. Aimee is concerned for her health and it's off to the vet. Goose is kept in overnight, the loneliness element working both for the pet alone and the owner missing her. But it's all good news and she soon returns home, albeit wearing a protective cone. Goose's views on the script requiring a visit to the vet are unrecorded, although Aimee confirmed 'She wasn't really cooperative' – everything fixed through the wonders of editing.

'Stuck In The Past' (Mann) (3:33)

This song was set in Houston, around a mission to Mars – which would be a one-way trip, as Aimee related to *Stereogum*:

I started thinking about that as the backstory of the song, where the person who volunteered had a family. Okay, you're married to somebody who is like,

'Yeah, I really want to go on a mission to Mars'. That feels like, 'You're going to commit suicide in front of me!'. That's crazy. That feels so sad. Would you try to talk the person out of it? Maybe you wouldn't, but you would regret not trying. The feeling of (this) song is like, 'I should have done something', and that regret is just so killer. You have hundreds of moments in your life where you're like, 'Why didn't I say something?'. Then the moment's over and it's too late.

This sense of regret comes through in these lines:

I had all this time while Houston dozed
Where I almost had a line composed
But the moment passed, the hatches closed

At heart it's a jaunty waltz, but with a melancholy edge. From the guitar-supported vocal, bass and strings fill out the sound, with lovely backing vocals from Paul Bryan and Ted Leo. Again, the sparseness of the arrangement is key – the impact of the strings as they sweep in, a thing of elegant beauty.

'You Never Loved Me' (Mann) (3:07)

The descending intro flows into a beautifully mournful verse, highlighted by a repeated 'You never loved me'. The falsetto backing vocals are soft but quite claustrophobic, bringing home the feeling of sadness, as does Bryan's wonderful string arrangement which gradually swells behind the almost funereal pace of the lead line. In an interview with *Consequence of Sound*, Mann said: 'I was really into this idea of background vocals, these ethereal *oohs* that were partly '70s easy listening, partly a little jazzy'.

She confirmed to *Billboard* that it's about a friend who got engaged and moved across the country to be with her fiancée, only for him to vanish and abandon her in a hotel room.

They just disappeared on her. It's certainly supposed to be a little bit wry and ironic and not entirely Boo hoo for me. I picture the narrator shaking their head and going, 'Wow. You really stuck it to me. Good for you'. I think sociopaths just don't have that fear that most of us have, where we live most of our lives going 'I hope this person likes me' or 'Is my loved one mad?' or 'How can I make this person happy, because it makes me happy?'. We are connected to other people in an emotional, underground kind of way, and I think they're just not.

These lines certainly set the scene:

Three thousand miles to sit in a room
With a vanishing groom
'til it undoes me.

Hermit crabs and atoms of unreactive helium analogise the isolation. Finally, the realisation comes that the 'vanishing groom' has actually done her a favour – 'And hey, when you're right, you're right'. It's a sad song but beautifully delivered, to the point where it almost becomes uplifting. Almost.

'Rollercoasters' (Mann, Jonathan Coulton) (3:44)

There's a lovely folk feel to the intro via the picked guitar. Melancholy floods through it like a delicate breeze, the thrill of the fairground analogy – 'You like how it feels, 'Round and 'round 'til you lose yourself in the air') shining through in a fragile way. Yet it's a much darker piece than the opening couplet suggests. As more detail is revealed, the spinning whirl where 'All those complicated deals, Your desperate appeals, Calling out to a god you know isn't there' is not the movement of fairground rides. Rather it appears to be the end-over-end descent of an out-of-control spacecraft, heading for destruction amid the forlorn screams of those on board. References to thin atmosphere and igniting boosters may be metaphorical, as Aimee has said of the song, 'You have those moments where you're just like, "Oh come on, please, just give me what I want. Do the thing I'm telling you to do!". You know it's not reasonable, you know it's not possible, but you just have those moments where you're just like, "Oh please!"'.

The simple rhythm and acoustic guitars, keep the mood. The chorus supporting vocal from co-writer Jonathan Coulton is exquisite, coupled with the accentuation of 'height', 'spite' and 'flight' in the bridge, moving the focus from controlled flight to terminal descent. The third verse is particularly enigmatic:

You were conjuring that year
A ghost engineer
Building gods who could put the clock in reverse

Amy said to *Guitar World*:

I wrote a few songs with Jonathan, who did a lot of background vocals and some fingerpicking guitar. He's a great songwriter, but also has this side that's cross-folky, finger-picky and (has) a love for the soft rock of the Seventies.

'Lies Of Summer' (Mann) (2:42)

Aimee confirmed to *Stereogum* that this partially fictionalised song 'was inspired by this guy I knew, a friend of a friend'.

It turned out he was bipolar, but also had some sociopathic stuff going on. We all found out some things that he had done and were really surprised – a lot of pathological lying. When you know someone like that, or find out something like that, a lot of stuff starts to become clear. Very confusing things in the past or confusing conversations start to make sense in light of that. You start to think, 'Oh, what about...'. A lot of the song is about rewinding through all of your past encounters with this person. It's definitely about an encounter with someone who is mentally ill in one or more ways. There's a lot of compassion to it, but it's also about trying to be realistic about what you're dealing with.

This led to another question regarding whether the subjects of her songs know that the songs are about them:

I don't tell them. Sometimes the songs are stuff that's completely made up. I always hope people don't really know that I'm writing about them. And of course, I've had people think I was writing about them even when I wasn't at all. That can be weird. They get really mad at me. It's easier just to disguise them in the song. Also, by the time they're in a song, the song has taken on a new life. The song is king, so if a song doesn't tend toward the topic you start out with, you just go with it. If it starts to change a little bit, that's fine. I think people tend to have these dynamics that get called up over and over in their lives that are particular to them. There are definitely times where I'm singing a song and think, 'Oh my god, this is exactly like this situation I'm in now', or 'This character is like this person I'm friends with now who's driving me crazy', or whatever. That happens way more often than not.

The song itself is laconic and easy-going as if the recounted lies no longer come as a surprise. Strings join for the chorus, and there's that feel of warm summer stillness, as Aimee sings knowingly:

We'll all rewind and just
Listen for the lies of summer

The arrangement of strings and piano is lovely, as are the backing vocals in the bridge, the result a striking and haunting song of awareness after the fact – the realisation that you don't really know someone that you thought you knew well, shining through:

If the doctor will just sign this pass
I put my hand up on the plexiglass
And scan your face, to see if you're in there
Wait a sec, I gotta write this down
'Cause once they put you in a paper gown
They leave no trace, like you've never been there

'Patient Zero' (Mann, Jonathan Coulton) (3:41)
The album's second single was written after Mann met actor, Andrew Garfield, at a party, before he became Spiderman in 2012. Speaking to *Guitar World*:

It was one of the first times he had been to L.A., and I got the impression he felt uncomfortable about it and the whole Hollywood experience. He seemed like a real artist and a more introspective person. Hollywood, with its rewarding of narcissism, is tough to people like that. So I wrote a song that was based on the idea of somebody with a lot of talent coming to Hollywood to star in a big movie and then having these disreputable forces working against him.

The song references the character, Carmen Sternwood, from Raymond Chandler's *The Big Sleep*. Philip Marlowe is hired to discover who is blackmailing her, but she is not who she appears to be. *Stereogum* considered Mann, a Chandler obsessive, to have much in common with the author. Both 'unsentimentally sentimental: tough-skinned and hard-boiled, but nursing the wounds of seeing people at their worst and living in a world gone bad'.

It's quite beautiful, indicative of Aimee's approach, the simplicity and the detail coming together in a wonderful song. It begins quietly, the strong vocal, supported by Leo and Coulton, describing the arrival of the new guy in Tinseltown – a budding star full of hopes and dreams, but unaware of how Hollywood works. He is Patient Zero, the first victim of a new viral outbreak. From the tentative opening, stately piano chords and plucked strings join in the second verse, the piano becoming more animated in the chorus as his confidence builds. The rhythm is subtle and easy, strings again a key feature, particularly in the bridge. The sour lyrical payoff – when he realises that the plum role was always going to someone else – returns us to the bare acoustic framework of the start, ending with an ominous piano chord. The arrangement swells in the final verse, an injection of power before slowing to twinkling piano and final guitar.

The video, directed and co-written (with Mann) by Daniel Ralston, is loosely based on Ronald Harwood's play *The Dresser* and features Bradley Whitford as the star of fictional play *The Hermit*, with James Urbaniak as his dresser. In the bittersweet plot, the dresser supports the star through his doubts about carrying off the role. The pair become friends, the star giving the dresser a hermit crab as a gift (inspired by the play). But when the play becomes a success, the now-lauded star drops the dresser for his new admirers (including a brief cameo from Aimee). The story jumps back and forth through time, starting and ending with the dresser releasing the crab into the ocean on a rainy beach – back to where the crab belongs, symbolic of the dresser's understanding that he doesn't belong in Hollywood either. It's a restatement of a favourite lyrical topic of Mann's, the pitfalls of the entertainment industry as a metaphor for life.

When asked by *Penny Black* if she enjoyed the process of making videos, she said:

No, I don't. Because so much of it is out of my hands. It's one thing to talk about something and picture it in your head, and you don't really know how the director is picturing it. And also I don't have much money, so you know, you're trying to do something – of course, I'm picturing this great piece of cinema in my head, you know – on $7,000. So, it's hard and kind of nerve-wracking and it's hard to know how it's going to come out. A lot of times it's about choosing a director that you trust, but that's hard, because it's hard to find people in the sweet spot of, 'Yes, making a video for practically free would be fun' and 'I know what I'm doing'. That's a very narrow demographic!

'Good For Me' (Mann, Jonathan Coulton) (4:09)

Again written with Coulton, it's full of fascinating lyrical phrases, a coolness coming from the unsettling situation of knowing that something isn't right, but carrying it forward anyway. 'What a waste of a smoke machine' is a great opening line, the theatricality set against the empty feeling once all pleasure has been excised with nothing to replace it. 'I pay when you go, But it only convinces me that you are good for me', suggests a controlling influence. The limited attention shown is not enough; the query directed as confirmation of her well-being:

Just a little bit of what I need
To soothe an appetite that I can't feed
Isn't that good for me?

The next verse speaks of clinical preparations and considered deniability, as obvious as any smoking gun, but 'I'll pretend I'm surprised by the lies that I'm telling to myself'. The final verse is an awareness that, under scrutiny, the singer creates further distress for herself by her unfocused clutching for approval:

And in the searchlight I can see
The rotors kicking up debris
The cloud, the dust, the blades are me

Sombre piano chords become more melodic into the verse, the bare structure adding pathos to the vocal, uplifting backing supporting in the chorus. Only later do the strings appear, adding warmth and colour, and it's a surprise when a simple drum rhythm appears. The mournful strings return, fuller, referencing the start with a sustained piano chord to end. It's heartbreakingly sad and beautifully arranged, the largely instrumental section at the end flooding in around the austerity of the piano.

'Knock It Off' (Mann) (3:01)

In the same vein as *Magnolia*'s 'Wise Up', it's a tough-love advice song:

This person's behaviour has just been so egregious. But after all his lies were revealed, he can't understand why his girlfriend broke up with him. Like, 'Why would you not trust me? I'm not getting credit for the ninety-nine times when I didn't lie!'. To me, that's fascinating, because that really is sociopath thinking. It's always a fresh new day, and (the sociopath) is weirdly present, but sort of too present, because they forget that the past has consequences in the present.

The song comes across as quite sad, but the back story is alluded to in the first verse with 'It made no difference what you told her, You say you're sorry but now what is that?', suggesting he is reaping what he sowed. 'You had your chances, but now they're gone', Aimee tells him – 'Oh baby, knock it off'. The second verse is brutally stark:

An overdose is almost clearer
A diagnosis is a mirror
You can't unsee it when you look like that

His continuing love is likely to remain unrequited and 'You can't just stand there on her front lawn, C'mon get in the car, it's over'. He could have had it all if he'd stopped the lies.

There's a lovely tone, the wordless intro seeing Aimee supporting herself with low and high harmonies. It's these that make the song shine, an acoustic guitar taking the bulk of the instrumental part early on, a beautiful string part coming in with the second chorus. It's a wonderful sound and it makes for a gripping song, sad but not maudlin.

'Philly Sinks' (Mann) (3:14)
Aimee wrote this for her last record, 'but it really didn't go'. Philly is a guy whose life is a rollercoaster of desolate times, parties and recrimination brought on by his drinking. The first verse sets the scene and his attitude toward women – don't get too involved and you won't get hurt.

It's always locusts, or floods, or drought
And then it's parties or prayer
He picks a girl he can live without
And puts her down over there

The chorus brings it all together with the effect alcohol has on his relationships: 'When he thinks he can't feel anymore .... And when he drinks, All the drunks hit the floor, And when he sinks you go down, And when you do, you both drown'. The variation in the second chorus changes the wording for the last three lines, noting that 'Philly drinks, At least he did when you knew him before'. And when he sinks, 'now the glass is a girl, But now the girl is a frown'.

The third verse takes a nautical tone. 'And if the rowing gets dull, Just knock a hole in the hull, And let the ocean swallow you down' is followed by another chorus variation where 'when he thinks he can't swim anymore, Philly drinks, Until the tide pulls away from the shore'.

It's another very sad song, with the knowing air of someone who has experienced the pitfalls of a relationship, soaked in alcohol. The guitar waltzes easily, picking out the bass line, as Aimee's voice is augmented by sighing harmonies in the chorus. Low strings sweep in for the second verse, lifting what is another inherently simple song.

'Simple Fix' (Mann) (4:12)
Consequence of Sound asked if she steps into a role when singing a song like 'Simple Fix', or if she has to detach from a personal perspective, Aimee explained:

> It's interesting. I do think that the very act of writing about it makes it a different experience for me. The tone of that song is very resigned. 'I guess we're just gonna do this forever. We're just going to keep having misread tensions.' You can feel the depression of the narrator in it. It's funny, because writing the song you build up to a chorus, and sometimes surprise yourself to hear what you're saying. When I came up with that chorus, it was very much a question that was posed to me. 'What is the simple fix?'. It's like, I think it's just 'Get out'. Get out altogether. That's the simple fix. Just walk away.

Strings start with an almost repeating sway, the circular bass line also tying in with the 'Here we go again' mantra. The repetition is beautifully controlled on a simple drum beat. A couple have become their 'worst mistakes', constantly at loggerheads, 'The rattles of two rattlesnakes, The antidote that no one takes'. Paul Bryan harmonises to create the two sides of the argument, a stalemate where neither of them can find the simple fix to end the torment, pig-headedly keeping at it: 'Let's call a spade a spade, I'm not going anywhere'.

Rattling piano adds tension, strings joining in counterpoint to the melody. It's a hugely engaging piece, delivered with elan, the easy charm disguising the trauma of a relationship in a very unhealthy place, the cyclical nature continuing into the outro. Fantastic song.

'Poor Judge' (Mann, John Roderick) (3:33)
The album ends with a song written with John Roderick from Seattle indie band, The Long Winters. Talking to *Consequence of Sound*, Aimee said:

> There is so much truth there. I felt that that song had a great melody, but also supports an idea that I can relate to. In a couple of other songs, I had written about the idea that you're trying to make a change, but you keep doing things over and over, and at what point in the cycle can I make a change? How do I make a change? What does a permanent change look like? I think that's a big problem for most people. They want to change, but they don't know how.

They can't see how the things that they're doing are still more versions of the same.

A rolling piano sets the pace for the opening verse's beautifully descriptive lines:

I rose like smoke, or the steam from your cup
A wave of heat where the lighter flares

Strings join the plaintive chorus, adding dynamic depth to the last line, building further during its reiteration:

You might have found some other reason
To burn me like a tissue screen
My heart is a poor judge
And it harbors an old grudge

The second verse takes the opposing view after the uplifting feeling of the first. It's further down the line and 'Falling for you was a walk off a cliff, A dream of a car with the brake lines cut'. Aimee and the strings work around each other into the bridge, and there's a Joni Mitchell/Carly Simon vibe, as she fights the opportunity to repeat her mistakes. But 'I'll say no, when you ask me ... 'Cause I won't let it past me ... til I see that I'm last and then', as we return to simple piano, Aimee exquisitely delivering the last lines, as the song – and the album – closes on piano alone.

Paul Bryan modelled his string arrangement on Paul Buckmaster's work with Elton John. Aimee noted, 'My theory about (Buckmaster's) arranging (is) that he arranges strings like a horn section. They often take the melody in unison, and they're very stabby and punchy, more horns than strings were arranged up to that point. So we looked to him for that song'.

Related Tracks
'Throw You Over' (Mann) (3:42)
The Japanese album release featured this bonus – a bit more upbeat than much of the rest, so probably perceived as an unconvincing fit. Piano and strings pick up a riff that Aimee develops, in a catchy and strong song with some interesting twists and striking elements. The bluntness of the 'I'm probably going to throw you over' line, is delivered with steely coolness – "Cause your heart is like a wheel, It'll turn and crush you under its heel'.

In the second verse, it becomes 'I'm probably going to hold you hostage' as 'Hope springs as eternal as hell', and in the third, 'I'm probably going to pull you under, 'Cause a love is not a kiss, And a win is not this shoddy near-miss, How sad that you drove me to this'. The chorus takes 'The Star-Spangled Banner' as a template, twisting it in an unexpected way:

Oh, say, can you see by
The light of my dreams
The delusions and the plotting and schemes
And if you could tell by
The rocket's red glare
You could see yourself that nobody's there

It ends with the opening piano riff. A fine song, but more deeply arranged and expansive, so may have unbalanced the album a little.

'Can't You Tell?' (Mann) (3:39)
In 2016, Aimee supported the *30 Days 30 Songs* campaign of musicians protesting Donald Trump's run for the presidency. The rhythm is easy, but with a locomotive texture from Abe Rounds' drums, Rusty Anderson's electric guitar the focal point. The lyric comes from Trump's perspective, pointing out his narcissism, self-aggrandising and bullying:

Though on the campaign trail the papers paint me like a clown
Still all I see are crowds who want to fit me for a crown
I point out all my enemies just so my fans
Bring them down

In a statement, Mann said:

I wanted to write about Trump in the first person because I think it's more interesting to speculate on what people's inner life might be. I had heard a theory that Trump's interest in running for President was really kicked off at the 2011 White House Correspondent's dinner when President Obama basically roasted him, so that's where I started.

There's a theory that he didn't think he could win, and didn't want to. 'Isn't anybody going to stop me?, I don't want this job, I can't do this job, My God!', followed by the killer jibe, 'Can't you tell, I'm unwell!'. You can sense the anxiety. To *Penny Black Music*'s suggestion that these lines almost make you feel sorry for Trump, she responded:

That was not my intention! I think the problem is, once I start writing a song and I try to connect to the person or the character I'm writing about, I find pathos in it, because I just think everybody's so pathetic. Everybody has this pathetic, sad side, that's just so – I mean, he's so fucking hopeless! Not to say that we should give him any more chances, but my God, I don't know what's wrong with him.

On his unorthodox campaign style and lies, we get 'I throw out any shit I want and no one trumps that card, So dazzled and distracted by your fantasy, Of Hildegard', referencing the visions of Hildegard von Bingen. It's a masterful put-down that cuts through to the heart of the matter.

'Avalanche' (Leonard Cohen) (5:13)

In June 2020, Mann's cover of Leonard Cohen's enigmatic song was used as the opening theme of HBO's *I'll Be Gone in the Dark*, which recounts the search for the Golden State Killer. It's a striking piece, Aimee's version retaining the atmosphere, pitched a tone higher and switching the frenetic rolling guitar for piano. Plucked guitars and strings fill out the sound, Aimee's voice rising majestically from the austere tones, with superb harmony support. It really is a fine reworking and was released as a single in September.

Coda

2018 began with Aimee making an appearance on comedy show *Corporate*, playing an employee with a desirable parking space. She doesn't sing, although 'Nothing is Good Enough' plays as her character is hit by a car. In February, she featured in an episode of *The Assassination of Gianni Versace: American Crime Story*, as a singer in a bar. After initially turning down the Phil Collins song she was asked to perform (still carrying scars from the Oscars, Aimee?), she provided a demo of The Cars' 'Drive'. The producers called it 'A little piece of musical genius'. She sang it alone on stage, beguiling, bringing the lead character to an emotional response.

For Record Store Day's *Black Friday* event on 27 November 2020, a double vinyl re-release of *Bachelor No.2* was issued in the US and Canada to mark the album's twentieth anniversary. With new sleeve art and limited to 4,000 copies, it was remastered and restored from the original session tapes and featured the thirteen-track US version with the addition of the five songs that had only been available on the *Magnolia* soundtrack album ('One', 'Momentum', 'Save Me', 'Wise Up' and 'Build That Wall') in a revised running order, with accompanying notes from Aimee for each song. Having recorded all the songs at the same time, 'it always felt like they should be on that record' as she told *Variety*. Plans are afoot to reissue *Lost in Space* in the same format. There is no firm information regarding a follow-up to *Mental Illness*, but it is apparently recorded and mixed.

Regarding her career – which has now been running for 40 years – Aimee said to *The Observer*:

I just love writing songs. There have been points where I've had writer's block and those feelings of 'I'll never write anything good ever again'. But at the end of the day, it's really fun to write, I love it and it's my favourite thing. I can't imagine ever getting tired of it.

There is definitely more to come...

Appendices

The Young Snakes

Gigging relentlessly around Boston after Aimee left Berklee, their 'Brains And Eggs' appeared on the *A Wicked Good Time* compilation, and in 1982 they released the only recording of their short career; the five-track EP *Bark Along with The Young Snakes*, on Ambiguous Records. In 2004, under the auspices of drummer Dave Brown, a compilation of fourteen tracks that didn't appear on *Bark Along*, appeared as *The Young Snakes featuring Aimee Mann*, on Lemon Recordings.

Even at this early stage, Aimee's sound is unmistakable, albeit with the addition of a bizarre operatic falsetto. Within the trio, her bass-playing is integral and interesting, the band proving themselves an impressive live unit with a funk that carried through into early 'Til Tuesday. It's not as experimental as some would suggest. The ethos is punk rather than the delivery, and there's plenty of melody amid some great playing. The songs on the EP are well thought out and delivered with elan, and it's almost a shame that they didn't continue, as I'm sure they would have produced some interesting music. It's an important recording in Aimee's career, showing elements that she would develop later, whilst evidencing the raw talent she already had.

We'll look at *Bark Along* first, and then the other tracks from the 2004 compilation, plus two 1981 demos. It seems that there might be another song called 'Enough', which I have not been able to locate.

Bark Along with the Young Snakes (1982)

'Give Me Your Face' (Mann, Vargas) (3:10)

With bass upfront from the start, and rough percussion in a laid-back funk, Aimee sounds confident and in-your-face, singing in a low key, the operatic flourishes coming through. It's a good song, driven by the bass figure, with nice guitar from Doug Vargas and interesting use of samba percussion.

'Suit Me' (Donnelan) (2:24)

More aggressive and punky, but still full of melody, Mann and Vargas share the vocals with a strong harmony to the end. There's drive from bass and drums, and it's more mature than might be expected – still holding up well today. The breakdown is both fun and interesting.

'Don't Change Your Mind' (Mann, Vargas) (2:53)

Another interesting one. Bass, drums and guitar work around each other in harmonious experimentation, before slipping easily into a finely melodic chorus. Vargas deploys harmonics to good effect, sliding into a brief textural solo. His backing vocals are good, again showing the band's maturity.

'The Way The World Goes' (Mann, Vargas) (1:51)

From a tentative start, the drums kick in with a great bass riff. Aimee's vocals are fantastic, pointed and forceful, with a hint of the delicacy we would come to expect. The instruments work well together, and there's melody throughout, driven by the drums.

'Not Enough' (Mann, Vargas) (2:48)

This mid-paced song has a strident structure, bass taking the riff while guitar moves around it. It's a great vocal, supported well in the chorus as Mann goes high. The pace picks up in the second half, with plenty going on. A great way to end what is a fine little record.

Related Tracks
'Brains And Eggs' (The Young Snakes) (3:32)

A stop/start intro moves into a sweeping guitar riff, becoming more erratic as Aimee starts to sing – bass as steady as a rock. The operatic flourish comes as a surprise, but it works. I can understand why she ultimately dropped it from her repertoire though! This is a high energy song and a good pick for their first release.

'Oh Nina' (The Young Snakes) (2:47)

From a barrage of drums, a driving riff emerges, over which Aimee sings at her most operatic. It's certainly unusual, but it suits the music. The bass is striking and carries much of the weight.

'Everything Goes Out Of Control' (The Young Snakes) (2:40)

This one crashes in with the chaotic intent of the title, Vargas singing some of the lead, sometimes in duet. One of the punkier songs, it's a full-on assault, but there's still melody, all coming to an ungainly end.

'Stop It' (The Young Snakes) (2:34)

A hint of the *Mission: Impossible* theme creeps in here, up-tempo and to the point with a robotic chorus. It would no doubt have been a great live number. Nice vocal-switching toward the end.

'Rewind' (The Young Snakes) (5:13)

By far the band's longest song, this one is all Vargas to start, until the rest of the band kick in and it coalesces. There's lots of energy, clashing guitars, and a decent structure, the vocals not appearing until halfway through – edgy punk flavours written all over it.

'Politics Are' (The Young Snakes) (4:02)

A clattering intro of percussion and harmonics leads into a stuttering song with well harmonised chorus, Aimee's vibrato deployed to good effect. There's a funky breakdown in the second half, driven by Brown.

'In This World' (The Young Snakes) (3:48)
The funk also comes through here in the exchanges between guitar and bass. The chorus is more laid-back, adding melody, but it's all about the structuring of the instruments. All the players have a place, and they deliver well, Vargas adding some excellent fills.

'Having Fun' (The Young Snakes) (4:08)
Scratchy guitar, leads in, Aimee reaching a bit for the deeper vocal parts. The chorus is very 1980s punk, and there's a theatrical texture. But it doesn't sound like Aimee is having as much fun as the title suggests. There's another interesting instrumental breakdown in the second half, with nice plucked bass.

'Gang X' (The Young Snakes) (2:03)
A frantic romp, with Aimee heading to operatic heights. It's disconcerting to those who know her from her later work, but great fun, and demonstrates how much more there is to her.

'Use Me' (Bill Withers) (3:23)
An unusual choice of cover, stripping the soul out of Bill Withers' original, replacing it with a punky funk. It's a snarly take, driven by the bass riff. Aimee uses her full range, and the intent comes through in spades.

'Karl K9' (The Young Snakes) (3:48)
This comes over like a mix of punk and 1950s TV themes. Aimee uses her stylised vocals throughout, supported by Vargas in the chorus. It's unusual, but the musicianship is excellent, and there's a fine instrumental breakdown in the second half, led by Vargas.

'Young Snakes' (The Young Snakes) (1:58)
The band's theme song? It's a battering instrumental statement of intent, with off-kilter weirdness thrown in from all three players, that no doubt opened many gigs in fine style.

'Brains And Eggs #2' (The Young Snakes) (3:36)
A live version of 'Brains And Eggs' with no major deviations from the original.

'Autistic' (The Young Snakes) (2:50)
The bass is plucked with vigour to introduce striking guitar chords and pounding drums. Again, Aimee sings the chorus with full support from Vargas.

'Me And The Girls' (The Young Snakes) (3:34)

A 1981 demo that doesn't appear on either of the releases. Driving drums and harmonic guitars, with Aimee in fine voice. A prowling piece with a good sense of dynamics, it stands up well. Some of the vocal extravagance sounds a little contrived, but then, they were!

'Just Like Christ' (The Young Snakes) (2:20)

Another 1981 demo, with more of an experimental approach. After the guitar intro, the bass riff kicks in, Aimee singing with real depth, particularly on the line 'Sometimes you think you're Christ-like'. Lots of good work from Vargas.

Compilations and Collections

Coming Up Close: A Retrospective (1996)

Released by Epic, this sixteen track 'Til Tuesday collection does the band justice over its 67-minute chronological selection. It includes 'Love in a Vacuum', 'Voices Carry' and 'You Know the Rest' from *Voices Carry*, 'No One is Watching You Now', 'On Sunday', 'Coming Up Close', 'Will She Just Fall Down', 'David Denies' and 'What About Love' from *Welcome Home* and 'Why Must I', 'The Other End (Of The Telescope)', 'J for Jules', '(Believed You Were) Lucky', 'Limits To Love' and 'Long Gone Buddy' from *Everything's Different Now*. Plus there's the previously unreleased 'Do It Again', recorded during the sessions for the last album and discussed previously.

Ultimate Collection (2000)

Released to cash in on Aimee's popularity after *Magnolia* and *Bachelor No.2*. The 20 tracks mostly comprise solo works from her major label days, with a few 'Til Tuesday songs in its 75 minutes.

This is a controversial one. Mann issued a statement confirming that she had no involvement, her offer to assist in putting it together 'flatly refused'. She went on to sue Universal Music Group over it, and politely side-steps fan requests to sign copies.

It is interesting as a rarities collection, rather than any kind of *ultimate* compilation. Of the meat-and-potatoes album tracks, we get 'Say Anything', 'Jacob Marley's Chain', 'Stupid Thing' and 'I Should've Known' from *Whatever*, 'You Could Make a Killing', 'You're With Stupid Now', Long Shot', 'Choice In The Matter', 'Amateur' and 'All Over Now' from *I'm With Stupid* and 'That's Just What You Are' from *Melrose Place*. 'Wise Up' from *Jerry Maguire* and 'Sign Of Love' from *Back To The Beach* appear, leaving the hard to find B-sides, 'Driving With One Hand On The Wheel', 'Take It Back', 'Baby Blue' and 'Jimmy Hoffa Jokes'. Finally, we get the 'Til Tuesday contingent of 'Voices Carry' (in its single mix), the title track from *Everything's Different Now,* and a live version of 'The Other End (Of The Telescope).

Aimee Mann (2003)

A near chronological run-through of solo highlights for the European market from BMG, with the slightly strange appendage of the opening track and the last three being 'Til Tuesday numbers ('The Other Side (Of The Telescope)', 'Voices Carry', 'What About Love' and 'Coming Up Close'). With nineteen tracks in all, the solo work features 'I Should've Known', '4th Of July' and 'Stupid Thing' from *Whatever*, 'Choice In The Matter' from *I'm With Stupid*, 'Build That Wall', 'Deathly', 'Wise Up' and 'Save Me' from *Magnolia*, 'How Am I Different', 'Red Vines' and 'Calling It Quits' from *Bachelor No.2* and a quartet of 'Guys Like Me', 'This Is How It Goes', 'Humpty Dumpty' and the title track from *Lost In Space*.

Other Appearances

1986 – Matthew Sweet – 'This Above All' (from *Inside*) – Backing Vocals
1986 – Cyndi Lauper – 'The Faraway Nearby' (from *True Colors*) – Backing Vocals
1987 – Scott Folsom – *Simple Talk* – Backing Vocals
1993 – Murray Attaway – 'Under Jets' (from *In Thrall*) – Backing Vocals
1993 – Desk – 'Astronauts' – Bass/Vocals
1997 – Duffy – *I Love My Friend* – Vocals
2000 – Goudie – 'When Will You Be Mine?' (from *Peep Show*) – Vocals
2000 – Michael Penn – *MP4 [Days Since A Lost Time Accident]* – Vocals
2000 – with Michael Penn – 'Reason To Believe' (Bruce Springsteen cover from *Badlands: A Tribute to Bruce Springsteen's Nebraska*) – Vocals
2001 – with Michael Penn – 'I Just Wasn't Made For These Times' (from *A Tribute to Brian Wilson*) – Vocals
2002 – John Doe – 'This Far' (from *Dim Stars Bright Sky*) – Harmony Vocals
2002 – Dan Zanes & Friends – 'Night Owl' (from *Night Time!*) – Vocals
2002 – 'Two Of Us' (with Michael Penn) and 'Lucy In The Sky With Diamonds' (Beatles covers from the *I Am Sam* soundtrack)
2004 – William Shatner – 'That's Me Trying' (from *Has Been*) – Backing Vocals
2004 – Jim White – 'Static On The Radio' (from *Drill a Hole in That Substrate and Tell Me What You See*) – Vocals
2004 – 'What The World Needs Now' (Burt Bacharach cover from *Sweetheart 2005: Love Songs*) – Vocals
2005 – Jim Boggia – 'Where's The Party?' (from *Safe in Sound*) – Backing Vocals
2005 – Bettye LaVette – 'How Am I Different' (from *I've Got My Own Hell to Raise*) – Vocals
2005 – Michael Penn – *Mr. Hollywood Jr., 1947* – Bass
2006 – Sierra Swan – 'Get Down To It' (from *Ladyland*) – Vocals
2006 – The Honeydogs – 'Ms. Ketchup And The Arsonist' (from *Amygdala*) – Backing Vocals
2007 – John Doe – 'Unforgiven' (from *A Year in the Wilderness*) – Vocals

2008 – Tim & Eric – 'Hearts' (from *Awesome Record, Great Songs! Volume One*) – Lead Vocals

2009 – The Decemberists – 'Engine Driver' – Vocals

2010 – Marc Cohn – 'No Matter What' (from *Listening Booth: 1970*) – Vocals

2012 – Steve Vai – 'No More Amsterdam' (from *The Story of Light*) – Vocals/Lyrics

2012 – Ben Gibbard – 'Bigger Than Love' (from *Former Lives*) – Vocals

2012 – 'Two Horses' (from *Tim & Eric's Billion Dollar Movie*)

2013 – Ivan & Alyosha – 'All The Times We Had' (from *All the Times We Had*) – Vocals

2014 – 'Come Sail Away' (Styx cover from *Community* soundtrack)

2015 – 'One Voice' (from *A Dog Named Gucci*) – Vocals

2016 – 'Yesterday Once More' (Carpenters cover from *Vinyl* soundtrack)

2017 – Kimon Kirk – 'Baby Who Knows' – Writer/Vocals/Acoustic Guitar

2017 – Mark Rivers – 'Everybody Bleeds' (from *Big Mouth* soundtrack) – Vocals

2017 – Game Theory – 'No Love' (from *Supercalifragile*) – Writer/Vocals/Drums/Bass

2017 – Ted Leo – 'Let's Stay On The Moon' (from *The Hanged Man*) – Vocals

Bibliography and References

A-Z Lyrics – https://www.azlyrics.com/
Aimee Mann in Print – http://www.aimeemanninprint.com/
Aimee Mann Official – https://aimeemann.com/
Album Liner Notes – http://albumlinernotes.com/
AllMusic – https://www.allmusic.com/
ASCAP.com – https://www.ascap.com/
AV Club – https://music.avclub.com/
Billboard – https://www.billboard.com/
Chicago Music Guide – https://chicagomusicguide.com/
Chicago Tribune – https://www.chicagotribune.com/
Consequences of Sound – https://consequenceofsound.net/
Fender Sixstring – https://fendersixstring.blogspot.com/
Genius – https://genius.com/
Guitar World – https://www.guitarworld.com/
Interview Magazine – https://www.interviewmagazine.com/
Jeff Raspe – https://unkajeff.wordpress.com/
Lyric Interpretations – https://www.lyricinterpretations.com/
Lyric Wiki – https://lyrics.fandom.com/wiki/LyricWiki
Mojo – https://www.mojo4music.com/
Musician, April 1993: 'Aimee Man – Sweet Revenge' – Mac Randall
Observer – https://observer.com/
Q Magazine – https://www.qthemusic.com/
Rate Your Music – https://rateyourmusic.com/
Record Collector – https://recordcollectormag.com/
Rock'n'Reel – http://www.rock-n-reel.co.uk/
Rock's Back Pages – https://www.rocksbackpages.com/
Rolling Stone – https://www.rollingstone.com/
SetlistFM – http://www.setlist.fm/
Song Facts – https://www.songfacts.com/songs/aimee-mann
Song Meanings – https://songmeanings.com/
Soundchecks – https://soundchecks.co.uk/
Spin Magazine – https://www.spin.com/
Stereogum – https://www.stereogum.com/
Stereo Society – https://stereosociety.com/
Steve Hoffman.tv – https://forums.stevehoffman.tv/
The Art of Process – https://maximumfun.org/podcasts/the-art-of-process-with-aimee-mann-and-ted-leo/
The Line of Best Fit – https://www.thelineofbestfit.com/
Til Tuesday.net – http://www.tiltuesday.net/
Time Out – https://www.timeout.com/
Unmask Us – https://www.unmask.us/
Varoom!, Winter 2009: 'Aimee Mann: Cover Me – Aimee, Gail and the illustrators' – Martin Colyer
Variety – https://variety.com/
YouTube – https://www.youtube.com/